MW00977562

Little Gifts
Of Joy

Sandra Wright

Sandra Mansfield Wright

Copyright © 2016 Sandra Mansfield Wright
All rights reserved.

ISBN: 1537645404
ISBN 13: 9781537645407
Library of Congress Control Number: 2016915281
CreateSpace Independent Publishing Platform
North Charleston, South Carolina

Dedication

This book of joy is dedicated to David Anthony Wright, my husband and joy, who died on February 18, 2015. Without him here, my joy was broken for a time, but he always told me, "Sandra Kay. Smile, shake it off, and go on," so I will. The quote, "You can cry because he's gone, or smile because he lived," (author unknown), spoke to me after his death. His memory and life make me smile, even laugh out loud often. He was my joy and my encourager. Because of him, this book was completed. He would be proud, and those who knew him know how much he liked to brag about those he loved!

Contents

CHAPTER 1

Attitudes of Joy

*E*very day, God gives to us a precious gift. For us, the challenge is to find the gift. If we notice and look for the gift, the little, or sometimes big, "*gift of joy*" in every day, we will find it! It is totally up to us.

There will be difficult days—hard, bad days—in each one's life, but I believe if one is in the habit of expecting and looking for the "*little gifts of joy*" every day, then even on those bad days, you can find the gift. It's there, hidden somewhere.

"So where do I look, or how do I go about this?" you may ask. See the joy in everything, everywhere, in every situation. Think on joy. When there is doubt, gloom, and sadness, make a conscious decision to think on joy instead.

Everyone seems obsessed with medication; there is a pill for everything. Rather than take a pill for depression, try taking joy instead. This attitude may help ward off other diseases caused by stress, worry, and depression. I am not saying medication is wrong; there are times when you may really need it. But practicing joy will always help.

Some say tension and stress are two of the biggest causes of illnesses in our country. If we will make a practice of looking for the "*little gifts of joy*" in our days, this alone can help relieve some of our tension and stress.

We must practice this daily, so as not to slide back into our old ways of dealing with problems and life in general. Practice going calmly along your way, looking for the "*little gifts of joy*" sprinkled in throughout your day.

Sometimes we take these "*gifts of joy*" for granted and let them slip right past us. They may be in a song we hear, in the smile of a child or loved one, a bird's song, church bells, the hug of a friend, a letter we receive, a good meal, a warm bed, or a bubble bath; anything that blesses us. Notice—stop and smile and take it all in. The time will pass, whether you pay attention or not, so notice and drink in every drop of it. This is your special "*little gift of joy.*" Unwrap it! Enjoy!

At the end of every day, make it a practice to write down at least one "*gift of joy*" you opened that day. I try and jot mine down throughout the day. When you start to become aware, you will see the gifts everywhere. It's fabulous, wonderful, and a gift in itself!

When we remain open to all our possibilities, there will be no stopping us. We will become a "*gift of joy*" to others because of our attitude of joyfulness and thankfulness. Have you noticed that people like to be around people who are happy? This is because we all desire to be happy. Well, we know if we have lived long enough, bad things sometimes happen. If we have developed this "*gift of joy looking,*" we will be better prepared to face even the days that are not filled with sunlight and birdsong.

Make joy all around you. Look for the good, because what good does dwelling on the bad do? Not one good thing! If you have bad in your life, pray, ask for help, do the best you can, and go forward with a smile on your face—even try to laugh out loud. Look even more closely for the *"gift of joy"* each day during this time. You will find it if you look and expect.

I have often been told when you are sad or down, get up, go out, and do something good for someone else. This is age-old advice, but still true. Think of doing for someone else as your *"gift of joy"* to them as well as to yourself. You cannot spread joy without getting some on yourself.

Never give up. Keep on keeping on. Hold your head up and move forward. These are all things we have been advised to do throughout our lives. These are true and time-proven bits of wisdom. I believe in these, but I have added the words "with a smile" to the end of each statement. Hold your head up and move forward—with a smile. Never give up—with a smile. It works. It really does.

Be optimistic, not grumpy, complaining, and fussy. People do not enjoy being around this temperament. The people who love you won't stop loving you because you are grumpy and sad, but they will eventually stop coming around you as often. They may feel an obligation to call you or come to visit you sometimes, but it will become less and less frequent. Those who don't love you will completely drift away. Who wants to be around a grumpy, sad, down person? No one.

You may say, "Well, I have good reason to be unhappy, sad, depressed, and down. This and that happened to me. Life was unfair, etc." While this may be very true, remember: people will cry with you for a while, but then they will start pulling away. They will only stay around and listen to sad and down for just so long. Then they will move on to be around joyful individuals because we humans gravitate to joy.

If you want friends and loved ones to come around—be joyful! Look for the "*gift of joy*," and then share your joy with them. When people ask you how you are, smile and tell them joyfully, "I'm just great!" Mean it, really mean it! More often than not, you will feel this way when you say it out loud. Because you have been unwrapping those "*little gifts of joy*" all day, you will mean these words.

> . . . . "Neither be ye sorry, for the joy of the
> Lord is your strength."

> - Nehemiah 8:10

CHAPTER 2

Joy Carriers

I remember, with great fondness, a dear lady whom I loved. In fact, everyone who knew her loved her. I was in my thirties when I first met her, and she in her late seventies. Ms. Beulah Phillips was her name. She was so full of joy, and she spent her days sharing that joy and doing for others. She never drove or owned a car, yet every morning she would get up, dress, put on her makeup, earrings and necklace, and get ready to go, just in case anyone came by and wanted her to go with them. On most days, someone did come by. On days when no one came, she would happily crochet something she was making as a gift for someone or cook one of her famous fresh apple cakes to give away. Even children and teenagers loved to be with her because she was "fun" and full of joy.

People, growing older is not the reason others don't want to be around you—they just don't want to associate with old (or young) grumpy, complaining, negative, or depressed people. Young and old alike will flock to you when you are filled with joy and have a loving, giving spirit. Ms. Beulah taught me this, and I still love her and smile when I think of her.

She was a great blessing and inspiration to my life when she lived. Ms. Beulah has remained a blessing even after her death, by her memory and all she represented—all the joy she shared with me and so many others.

Ms. Beulah was not rich, not even well-off. She had been a widow since her forties and lived in a government-subsidized housing area much of the time I knew her. She had known sorrow, heartache, and hard times, but she never talked about this or dwelt on it. There was always a smile on her face and joy in her heart! Friends were never lacking. Loneliness wasn't in her vocabulary because she didn't allow herself to be lonely.

She would call me and say, "Sandy, I want you to come and get me on Tuesday, and we will have lunch at such and such restaurant. Then I want you to take me to see Ms. so and so." I would answer "yes Ma'am" because I knew we would have fun together. Then she would say, "I have made you a fresh apple cake; come by and get it." Or, if she saw I was really busy with something, she would say, "Pick me up, and I am coming over to help you." She would see a need and meet it, always willing to help others.

A great example of how to live joyfully and fully each day was exemplified by her life. Don't sit around feeling sorry for yourself. Get up and do something for someone else. There are people everywhere who need your help and encouragement. Look for them. Open your eyes and see them and be a "*little gift of joy*" to them.

One of the best ways to keep joy in our life is to serve others. By getting outside of ourselves and thinking of others, we become more fulfilled and joy-filled. By giving of ourselves, we receive much in return. Notice others—their needs, their hurts, their joys, and their accomplishments. Laugh with them, as well as cry with them. Be thoughtful and caring, giving and loving. If we care, we may be hurt. This is a truth I have found through life, but your joys will also be deeper by caring. Give of yourself. Serve others with joy. When you assist others, you bring joy to them as well as to yourself.

Young women need older women to teach them, to encourage them. The same is true for men. Be there for someone today. Look for opportunities to be a *"gift of joy"* to another in your life. See a need and meet it. Open your eyes and your heart.

Another story that comes to my mind is of an aunt by marriage, Aunt Stella. When I would go to visit her, she would be so thrilled and tell me how much my coming meant to her. She would talk graciously about me taking my time to see her, as if I had done something wonderful for her. While we talked, she would make me feel so loved and special. I always loved visiting her, and I now remember her with a smile. She was gracious, loving, giving, and always kind.

Some older people you go to see them start the minute you walk in. "Well, it's about time you came. It's been months, etc.," and they make you feel bad as soon as you enter their house or room. For the entire stay they fuss, complain, and criticize. You sit there thinking to yourself, "Have I been here long enough to leave?" You can't wait to get out of there, and then it is even longer between visits the next time. You want to be around joyful, loving people—everyone does. Remember this, and do not allow yourself to become the complaining, fussy old bitty. Don't do it—ever!

Joyfulness is contagious. You can spread your joyful spirit. You can! Just as being around grouchy, negative people is contagious, so is joy! Be a "carrier" of joy, and smile as you do it. You can make a difference in your world if you have the desire and determination to do so.

Some people, when they are sad and hurting, may seem to not appreciate joyfulness. I am not talking about being disrespectful of sad times. You will know when to be caring, kind, and sincerely touched by others' grief or pain. But a loving, caring, gentle, joyful spirit will help pull them through.

> "Weeping may endure for a night, but joy cometh in the morning."
>
> - Psalm 30:5

> Weep with them—laugh with them, too!
> Most of all, love and care.
> "We cannot cure the world of sorrows, but we can choose to live in joy."
>
> - Joseph Campbell

As I said before, when we care and notice, we may hurt, but we cannot allow hurt to overcome our joy. We must continue to think up positive, uplifting, encouraging thoughts and allow our spirit of joy to glow. You are here in this world to shine your own light. Shine . . . laugh . . . lighten up the room. Be joyful in your heart, and that joy will beam in your face and eyes.

Mark Twain said, "Wrinkles should merely indicate where smiles have been."

Smile a lot, so that when you grow old, your face will light up with the softness and radiance of a joyful, loving, kind, and happy person who thought on joy, rather than be a frowning, negative, sad, hard person. Your thoughts really do make a difference.

You can find joy if you look for it every day. You can change the way you think, and only you can do this.

> "The gloom of the world is but a shadow; be-
> hind it, yet within our reach is joy. Take joy."
>
> - Fra Giovanki

Share your joy with others. Be up, going, doing, and helping those around you. When you walk into a room, carry your joyfulness with you. Share it freely with others. Remember, people love to be around happy people. Make good time for yourself. This is not selfish. When you feed your soul and your joy, you will have something to give to others in your life. Your soul and spirit will not be poor. Be lively, be courageous, be invigorating, be alive, be well, and joyful! These attitudes will spill over from your life and splash onto those around you. Rejoice every day! Live your life joyfully, and be a joy-spreader today and every day. Encourage, uplift, and love; always love.

> "There is nothing more beautiful than cheerfulness in an old face."

> - Jean Paul Richter

Our choices determine our lives! Choose wisely. Choose joy. Make it your habit to be joyful. When you major your attention towards joyfulness in every situation and every choice, the outcome will be different.

> "Everything can be taken from a person but one thing: the last of the human freedoms— to choose one's attitude in any given set of circumstances, to choose one's own way."

> - Viktor Frankl

You are responsible for your own actions. No one else is responsible for your actions. We choose how we react in every situation. If we are in the habit of being joyful, situations will affect us differently. Negative draws negative;   positive draws positive.

"If you don't like something, change it. If you can't change it, change your attitude. Don't complain."

- Maya Angelou

"Get over it!" Bad, unfair things often happen in life. How one deals with these either makes them better or worse. We often bring more sorrow and unhappiness on ourselves by our own attitudes and choices. Choose today, right now, to be joyful inside anyway—no matter what. Hold your head up, smile, and go forward! Blaming someone else doesn't help. Being unforgiving doesn't help. In fact, this only serves to destroy your joy. Let go. Change the situation, or change your attitude and perspective about the situation. Incline your mind toward joy and move on!

When you think on joy, you will bring more joy to yourself. Notice all the good that happens in your life. Think on this. Major on the joy! What gives you joy? What brings you pleasure? Who do you enjoy being around? Spend your time with these people and these things. When you are looking for joy, you will find it. Look for it! Become a joy carrier!

CHAPTER 3

A Joyful Groove

*J*oyful habits are good for your health. Be careful where you place your attention in life. I have read that our brains form trenches or grooves as we think in certain ways. Thinking negative thoughts can deeply entrench our brains. People tend to think pessimistically more often than positively, so we have to make a special effort to get out of this harmful brain rut and think joyfully instead. We have to train our brains to make new grooves—a "joyful groove."

One of my grandsons, when in kindergarten, came in with his report card of pluses and minuses. He had twenty or more pluses and one minus. The only thing he told me was, "I have a minus." He didn't notice all those great pluses. To his mind, he had failed. We all tend to be like this in life. We can do most everything right, but do one thing wrong, and we beat ourselves up over and over. People may compliment us all day long, but let one person say one negative remark, and we are crushed. This is because our minds are grooved in negative thoughts more than positive thoughts.

I have heard it said that it takes ten positive statements to overcome one negative statement, and I have found this to be so true. With this said, we should all be very careful to encourage and uplift one another, and try to only say positive words to others—especially to children.

> "Those who bring sunshine into the lives of others cannot keep it from themselves."

> - J. M. Barrie

We are often hard and unforgiving of ourselves. Give yourself a break. Lighten up. Be joyful and forgiving. Give yourself cause to celebrate life today. Think on joy. Be joyful because you are alive. You are blessed with this day to find the "*little gifts of joy*" throughout the day. Look for them, and you will notice them!

For very practical people who find this philosophy too light, please think on this. To choose to be optimistic is not simply burying your head in the sand and pretending everything is wonderful and problems do not exist. It is an attitude that believes we can make a positive difference when we choose optimism rather than negativism, because ultimately, what good does thinking negatively do? By thinking positively, we can possibly change the situation for the better. Simply put, it will make us feel better!

> "We shall never know all the good that a simple smile can do."
>
> - Mother Teresa

Find your joyful groove and make it your habit to get into it daily, starting today! Determine to do this now.

CHAPTER 4

Why I Wrote This Book

Paint pictures in your mind
Of things you want to see,
Of places you want to go.
And dream in blissful sleep
And wake to find them so.
Only you have your dreams.
Only you can make them true.
Why wait till someday—
Do it now—Go!

- Sandra Mansfield Wright

Most of us don't pursue our dreams because we are afraid. We are afraid we will fail, afraid of the costs in money and in time, afraid of what others might say or think, etc.

"Who has begun has half done. Have the courage to be wise. Begin."

- Horace

When I started to write this book, I really didn't want to tell anyone because I thought others would think, "Who is she to write a book," or "how silly"—and on and on my mind would go in doubting thoughts. I have no credentials or fame in my background, so who am I to write on the subject of joy? None really, except that my heart told me to write. I love to write. I feel fulfilled when I am writing. I love to read books that help me, that lift me up. Others' writings have encouraged, uplifted, and helped me through the years, so I wanted to write myself. One of my main reasons for writing was that I sought for my grandchildren to know me more fully, know my feelings, who I am at my very core. I wanted them to read this someday and feel they know something about their grandmother.

I loved my grandmother, but I didn't really know much about her except surface things. Of course, the most important thing was that she loved and accepted me. That was the main and most important thing for me to know. I knew she was a hard worker who helped run a dairy farm, kept a farm- house, was a great cook, and went to church every week. The one piece of advice I remember her giving me was to never be lazy.

A cousin called me one day and told me about his search for our family's history. He was so excited about all he had found and shared much of that with me. He told me about our great-great grandfather: his name, when and where he was born, where and when he died, and where he was buried. After we finished talking, I thought, "How sad that we know nothing about the man—what he felt, what he thought, who he really was."

When people die after a generation or two, everything about them is gone, unless they did something extraordinary in the world or wrote down their thoughts and ideals.

There was such a desire in me to write, so I wrote. Whether this book will ever get published or not, I don't know. Someday I hope some of my descendants will read it, and pray it may make a difference and help them or someone else, as books have helped me.

My husband, David, wrote several books, and his first book, *River Rock*, was praised by many people. Everywhere we went, people would ask him, "Now when is your next book going to be ready?" His books are fictional and totally different from mine, and they are good and fun to read. I felt if mine were published—being so different from his—people would never say things like that to me, and I would be discouraged. Then I realized my book is not the same type as his, and mine will have a totally different reader. Most everyone enjoys David's books. Mine may not appeal to everyone, but hopefully there will be those who do like it.

I told myself, "The main thing is to write what you think, what you feel, and just write." As I always told David, "Even if no one buys your book, at least you have written a book. How many people can say they have actually written a book?" So I'll go for it!

You will never become old if you continue to use your brain and keep thinking and doing—I hope. Stretch yourself and push yourself outside of your comfort zone. Try something new and exciting. Never stop. Never give up. Be up, going, and doing—hopefully doing things that will bless others around you. Pay attention to what your heart tells you to do. Be open to opportunities, and be ready to go for them. Don't worry or be afraid of what others will say or think. Be more concerned if you don't go for your dream. At the end of our lives, it will be better to say "I did it" than to say "I wish I had tried that." To stretch and grow is a good thing!

> "What you have accomplished pales in comparison to what you can do with your talents now."
>
> - Alexandra Stoddard

> "You are equipped for whatever you are passionate about accomplishing. Do something gutsy, bold and noble."
>
> - Alexandra Stoddard

Alexandra Stoddard is one of my favorite authors, and I've read every book she has published. If you find a writer you love, you know what I'm talking about when I say, "I am so excited when anything new she has written comes out." I go buy it, sit, and relish every word. I quote her often and hopefully have not plagiarized anything of hers, but I have read her so often that many of her ideas have inspired me. She is a kindred spirit, and I agree with most of her philosophy —not all, but most.

I have found it helps me to find authors I love to read and books on subjects I enjoy. It encourages me when I am at a low period. It helps me begin a project by motivating me. It inspires me to do.

One of my sons-in-law loves to make fun of my "silly little quotes" and my "happy spirit." There is a chalkboard hanging in my house on which I write quotes and sayings. After he has been at the house, I will often find the quote changed. For instance, one quote I had written was, "One only becomes old when we allow regrets to replace dreams." He changed it to read, "One only becomes old when we allow rug rats to replace dreams." I always get a smile or a laugh from his rewritten quotes. I know he is looking forward to reading this book! Like I said before, "this book isn't for everyone." He is very supportive, and I am sure he will read my book—even if it's not his type of book.

I believe you should go for what you are passionate to do, be it writing, painting, hiking, mountain climbing, or whatever you love. I am passionate about writing, so I am writing! I do so hope you will enjoy this book, and that it will encourage and uplift you!

CHAPTER 5

Don't Worry—Be Joyful

*"Every morning I spend fifteen minutes filling my
mind full of God, and so there is no room left for
worry thoughts."*

- Howard Chandler Christy

I find what you worry about often comes to pass. If you
fear the worst, it will often happen. When you start
to worry, quickly see that thought as worry and change it to
joyful, grateful, thankful thinking. Difficult situations and difficult
people can teach us great lessons, if we will allow it. This
is worth repeating. Difficult situations and difficult people can
teach us great lessons if we will allow it. I have heard it said
that problems only come to make us stronger, better people!
Sometimes I don't want to be any stronger. How about you? I
feel I have had enough problems, but that is life. So we have to
make the best of it and go forward with hope.

"The art of living lies less in eliminating our troubles than in growing with them."

- Bernard M. Baruch

As long as one lives, there will be worries and problems. But the trick is not to allow the problems and worries to get inside you and eat at you. Put them in their proper place.

"Go to sleep in peace. God is awake."

- Victor Hugo

"You have to take it as it happens, but you should try to make it happen the way you want to take it."

- Phyllis Bottome

"Do you know why that cow looks over that wall? ... She looks over the wall because she cannot see through it, and that is what you must do with your troubles—look over them and above them."

- German Proverb

"Life is not always what one wants it to be, but to make the best of it, as it is, is the only way of being happy."

- Jennie Jerome Churchill

"A happy woman is one who has no cares at all; a cheerful woman is one who has cares but doesn't let them get her down."

- Beverly Sills

Don't allow your troubles to get inside you and get you down. What is within you shines out from your eyes, your very being. Be calm. Be at peace. Be joyful.

"I am determined to be cheerful and happy in whatever situation I may be, for I have also learned that the greater part of our happiness or misery depends on our disposition and not on our circumstances.

- Martha Washington

"Keep a green tree in your heart and perhaps a singing bird will come."

- Chinese Proverb

We all need to lighten up and not take things so seriously. Flow with life. Bend, don't break. Laugh out loud every day. I have found this to be one of the best medicines for what ails you. Laughter! This is very important. Laugh out loud every day— even if you have to fake it. Do it. It really makes you feel better; trust me on this. Really. Find someone who makes you laugh and be around them as much as you can. Read something funny. Watch funny movies. Whatever it takes, find something to make you laugh, and learn to laugh easily. Oh, and I have also read that laughter makes you lose weight, too. Hip-hip-hooray!

Learn to wait. A saying, "What is, is" comes to my mind. We cannot always change things. What is, is! And what happens, happens! Some things happen that are not good, and we don't like it and don't want it to happen, but it does anyway. Often we may feel overwhelmed with life's problems, but we must not allow these issues to defeat us. Keep on top of your troubles.

Everyone, no matter who they are, has problems. When I was young, I would look at someone and think they had it all. I'd be envious of their wealth, their beauty, their lifestyle— whatever it was that I felt was better than what I had. But as I matured, I realized every human being has difficulties, doubts, fears, and failures. They are a common bond of the human race. Some have more trials than others, that's for sure. But we all have worries and concerns.

It is how we deal with the troubles that often makes them more difficult on us. If we dwell and obsess on them, they seem to get worse. This is why I say "rise above your problems."

I recently read a quote from the writer of *The Purpose Filled Life*, Rick Warren, who said, "You are either going through a problem, coming out of a problem, or will have a problem soon." This is just life. Everyone, let me say this again: everyone has problems. It is how we handle these that either makes us or breaks us.

You may see people who seem to have the "perfect" life, and you don't see them ever having any difficulties. Believe me, they have them—everyone does. It's just that possibly they have learned to rise above their troubles and worries by their thinking.

How you think about your issues can make them last longer, grow darker, or help you to raise your spirit above them and carry you through them.

I have found faith to be a great help in times of trouble. Studies have shown that people who have great faith are more resilient. I have heard some say, "Faith is a crutch." By definition, a crutch is a very good thing when you are unable to stand alone. Using a crutch when you are broken is no sign of weakness, but rather, just good common sense. When you would fall on your face without its help, it is good to have a crutch. So having faith is not something to be ashamed of; it's a great help and strength in times of troubles.

Your attitude can make all the difference in your situation. Cry, if you must, then wipe your eyes, put on your best, most favorite outfit, wash your face, brush your hair, and try to get out of yourself and think on something or someone else. Think uplifting, joyful thoughts, and say these aloud to yourself and to others.

My husband, David, made me laugh so often. This is one of the things I loved most about him. He gave me laughter and joy. My grandchildren make me laugh often, too. Notice what causes you to laugh and go for it. There are certain people who bring laughter into your life. Make it a point to be with them. Always be around people who bring joy to your life.

Think on good. Think interesting thoughts. Do not allow boredom to settle into your days. Get up and fight against it with every fiber of your being. Don't let the blues keep you down. This is your life to live, so live it up and get going and doing!

Depression and boredom can be chased away when we do for others. There are always people who need your help, your care, your love, and your encouragement. Find your niche in life—what you love to do—and then do this for those around you. I believe every person has a talent, a gift some might call it. Oh, you may think you don't have any talents or gifts, but I know you do. Most of the time it is something you enjoy doing: cooking, sewing, gardening, reading, writing, singing, playing music, cleaning, organizing, planning events, flower arranging, knitting, accounting capabilities, corporate expertise, and on and on it could go. Anything you do can be given as help to others. You can volunteer your time to an individual, group, or event. Just open your eyes and heart to the needs of those around you and be there for them.

"The best use anyone can make of any day is to enjoy it—and then spread that joy to others. Let us celebrate today!"

- John Kremer

Make it your habit, your practice, your goal in this life to enjoy today and celebrate it in ways that bring joy to yourself as well as to others. Every day holds a "*little gift of joy*," and some days even bigger gifts of joy. Even on the tough days, the rough days, or the sad days, if we will expect and look for our "*little gifts of joy*," we will find them. Today I saw yellow butterflies, fluttering all around in my back garden. They were a sudden and delightful "*little gift of joy*" to me today. Make yourself notice the things that go on around you. Open yourself up to all there is.

"When sorrows come, remember that you have experienced joy and will again."

- Alexandra Stoddard

The above is one of my favorite quotes. Sorrows do come to all of us at some time. We must remind ourselves that joy will come again. This is difficult when you are hurting, isn't it? This is a life lesson, and a hard one. Try to think up and on joy because what we think affects us and everything we do. When you are down, think up and up will come! Always come back to joy. Begin with yourself. Work on yourself. Look on the bright side of everything.

"Pain is inevitable, but misery is optional."

- Tim Hansel

We can choose to live through our pain, learn from it, and grow, or we can choose to live in misery. But it is our choice to make. Living in misery will not only hurt us, but it will hurt all those around us, as well as our loved ones and friends. Eventually, misery will drive them away from us. If you want to be alone, dwell in misery. You can change your attitude and change your life always.

> "If I were asked to give what I consider the single most useful bit of advice for all human-ity, it would be this: Expect trouble as an in-evitable part of life and when it comes, hold your head high, look it squarely in the eye, and say, "I will be bigger than you. You cannot de-feat me."

- Ann Landers

If we live long enough, we will have troubles, but still know that life is good and worth living. It is beautiful, rewarding, and glorious, and there is much, so very much to enjoy. Look for the good. Look for the joy and stay in a place above your troubles. Go in your mind to a beautiful, happy place often.

My David's death was the hardest thing I have ever had to face so far in my life. It was totally unexpected and sudden.

One day I had him in my life, happy, and the next morning, he was gone from my everyday life. Just like that, much of my joy went away. It devastated me because my life was wrapped up in him. There was grief, sorrow, loneliness, emptiness, panic, fear, worry—all the emotions one feels at the death of a dear loved one. I came through, and I'm still coming through this awful time with the help of family, friends, God, love, and hope. I write this so others will know that they, too, can live through the sorrows of life. I will not say it is easy, because it is not. But it is possible. You can smile and laugh again, day-by-day, as you keep looking for the "*little gifts of joy*" in each day the Lord gives you. You can and will breathe again—not with the same joy, but a quiet joy will come in the morning. My love for David did not die but goes on, and I remember him with a smile and lots of laughter. That's what he wanted, and that's what I will do. I'll remember him with joy always!

CHAPTER 6

Slow Down, You're Moving Too Fast

*L*ife is just too precious to be too serious, nervous, always rushing without taking the time to stop and ask yourself why. Where am I rushing to? Why am I rushing so? What is the hurry? Often we rush so fast that we actually miss our life, our minutes, our hours, our days, weeks, months— yes, years. I know, here is another person saying, "Notice your moments." But it is true and worth repeating again and again. If you don't notice this moment, it will be gone anyway, never ever to return.

"Rush never!" This philosophy will help you have a more joyful life. One of the things that robs us of our joy is rushing—running in different directions and feeling scattered and stressed, pulled here and there. Trying to do too many things, multi-tasking, and always pushing yourself to get your days more crowded will rob you of your joy. Whenever we try to do too much, we damage ourselves and often hurt those around us. Just know you cannot—and should not—do everything! When we are scattered, we don't do anything well. When we try to do too much, too fast, we lose the fun, the joy in the doing. There is always time to do what is really important. Find your joy again by finding what is major to you, and then put your time and effort into that.

When you take time, you will gain so much in return. You may have artistic talents: writing, painting, poetry . . . talents that may surface when you take time to get to know yourself and your loves. No one who is rushing all over the place in every direction can ever truly find their whole talents, their purpose, their full joy. Relax, slow down, breathe and relish the moment. Make this your motto.

Think on who and what is most vital to your life. Make a list of the people or things that are valuable to you. Then notice these. Make time for yourself. Do not allow trifles; things or people who are unimportant to you take up all your precious, joyful time on this earth. Reevaluate your priorities.

Happiness and joyfulness depend on ourselves.

"I am happy and content because I think I am."

- Alain Rene Lesage

"Joy is not in things; it is in us."

- Richard Wagner

We—at least most of us—have to work to pay bills, keep our houses clean, wash clothes, help feed and cloth others, and do things that aren't always what we would call "fun" or "joyful."

But many of these things we must do are made better with a joyful and thankful spirit. If you can, do something you love to make a living, but if you aren't there yet, then do those things as a hobby or as volunteer work. You may be an artist who works in an office by day to pay your bills. What's important is to find your joy!

A woman from a third world country was speaking to a group of ladies, and something she said has stuck with me through the years. She said she was always thankful every time she washed dishes because that meant she had fed her family one more time. Her children had eaten food and were filled, not hungry. That statement certainly gave me a new perspective on the chore of washing dishes. We should be thankful, so very thankful for many of the blessings we take for granted every day. Look with new eyes at things you may have once thought of as chores and dull work.

America has so much, and often it takes tragedy or natural disasters to wake us up to things we don't always notice and appreciate. If we take time and watch for those "*little gifts of joy*" in our days, we won't miss as much.

As I was writing this, I received a call from my sister, who lives in Kentucky. She only had a quick moment to tell me they were okay. I had been unable to reach her for two days due to a severe ice storm. All their phones were out; there was no power, and no water. They found a neighbor who had a generator and used her phone to let me know they were all right, although the area was declared a natural disaster site. Now three days ago when I spoke to her, there were no problems.

They had no idea something like this would happen. Life was moving along as usual. After going through this, the simple things such as running water, a hot shower, hot food—just the everyday things we take for granted—will be more precious and treasured to her, as well as to me. I know it caused me to give a special prayer of thanks for my comforts, the simple comforts that I so often take for granted. They are wonderful blessings. We should never whine and complain, but rather <u>slow down and notice</u> all we have—all our blessings—because <u>our whole world can be changed in an instant</u>.

CHAPTER 7

Make Your Own Joy

*N*ever look to others to make you happy. You are responsible for your own happiness, and in the same vein, you are not responsible for anyone else's happiness. You cannot make anyone else be happy. Oh, you can for moments, but not for a continued time. I've seen people who try to buy things to make everyone around them happy. You can love and encourage your loved ones, lead them, and show them by example, but you cannot make them be happy. We feel guilty when our loved ones aren't happy, don't we? I know. I have certainly been there many times. We all may learn a valuable life lesson by going through a problem, and we cannot—and often should not—fix our loved ones' problems. We can and should pray for them and always love them, but we can't always fix everything for them.

A wise person once told me, "Even God had trouble with His kids, and He was a perfect parent." Think about this. It's true, you know. This will help you as a parent, so write it down somewhere and read this statement often.

One of the most difficult things for me, as a mother, to get into my mind is the fact that if my children aren't happy and joyful, it's not necessarily my fault. Women tend to always feel guilty about something—about everything! We must tell ourselves over and over, until we believe it, that we are not responsible for our grown children's' happiness. Men may have this problem, too. I only know how I, as a woman, feel. We can pray for our children to be happy. We can love them and try to be as helpful as we can, but we cannot make them happy. In the same way, we can't blame our parents if we aren't happy. There comes a point in everyone's life when we must take responsibility for our own life, our own happiness, our own choices and actions. We choose to be joyful or sad in our spirits. Joy is the high road. Take joy! It will make your life much easier to manage. A joyful spirit eases the way by its mere presence. Our happiness, our joy is totally up to us. It is our responsibility. The main way to find joy and have joy in our lives is to think joy, nurture joy, and be mindful of the way we think. Make joy a habit.

> "One must put all the happiness one can into each moment."

> - Edith Wharton

> "Write it on your heart that every day is the best day in the year."

> - Emerson

We can train ourselves to be joyful every day. We can make ourselves aware and notice the good all around us. There are simple, wonderful pleasures in our everyday life, if we will notice them.

With spouses, what can I say? If you are happy and full of joy yourself, this is the best you can do. It is your responsibility to try and make your home a place of peace and joy, but if you are married, there are two people. It is wonderful and such a blessing if you can do this together. The greatest gift you can give your children is to be joyful yourself. Joy spreads. Love and scatter joy all around you!

Be grateful and be joyful! Try to make the world a better place each day by doing something good, something kind, and something loving for another person. Every day, notice and make a point to do at least one good thing for someone else. This one act can really make a difference in the world—one act at a time. You will find that once you start doing this, you will feel so full of joy that you will want to do more than one thing per day. You will be looking for ways to do more and more. That is great! The world can use more good deeds, can't it? And you will not only be helping fill the world with joy for others, you will be filling yourself with more joy. Smile and go for it. It's a good thing; it really is. This becomes such a rich blessing and a way of life—a joy-filled life!

There is good in growing older. We understand a bit better now how things that we once considered major issues just really weren't! As parents, we often take things way too seriously and say no to things we sometimes should just let go.

The one piece of advice I would give a young parent is to let some things go. A little dirt is good for kids; it will help their immune system. The teenage years will pass. Lots of the things that distress us so are just a phase, natural growing pains. It will pass! Save your no's for big and important issues. Remember, "She (he) who laughs—lasts," so laugh, don't cry, and always love them. Always love them. Always love them!!! As a parent, you won't do everything right. You will probably make many mistakes, but do your best, pray a lot, and laugh a lot. As long as you love your children and grandchildren and show them your love that, to me, is the most important thing. If you love them, you will say no sometimes. You won't always be popular with them, but through it all, you will be there for them. Time means love. Spend time with them—quality, good time. Share moments of joy with them. Make memories that will last a lifetime together.

Sometimes in families there may be major problems where a simple "love them" and "always be there for them" just won't be enough to get you through. Your family may be in major turmoil with drugs, alcohol abuse, pregnancy, physical and emotional abuse, or mental issues. Loving them and being there for them may be difficult; it may be downright impossible for you right now. We don't stop loving someone because they are unlovable or because they have hurt or disappointed us. We may not be able to be around them, either, because it is emotionally bad for us or for them. Their behavior may be totally unacceptable for us to deal with at this time. I am not a professional and cannot, and will not, give advice here. There are times when we may need to turn to professionals to help us through, or we may need to join a support group. Faith and prayer helps. Keep praying—keep on praying!

CHAPTER 8

Stormy Days — Sunny Days

Remember, everything you think affects your spirit, your attitude, your being. Joy is a result. Sorrows and bad times—moments that are not full of joy— come in life. Remember what joy feels like, and look for it to come again! Nothing in life is perfect, but you can make it better by how you choose to react. By understanding what is important to you, you can weather the storms of life and come out on the sunny side.

In nature, there are sunny days, rainy days, thunderstorms, and quiet, beautiful, blue-sky days. It is the same in our lives. There will be good times and bad times. Just as the sun will pop out after the storm, so will good come again in our lives. Appreciate the joyful days, and weather the storm on the bad days.

Your spirit, whether joyful or sad, affects those around you. Do you want to be a carrier of joy or gloom? You have this choice to make each day. Choosing joy can make you healthier and definitely happier. What you think, you become. It is your choice. Why would anyone consciously choose to be unhappy, grumpy, and sad? I just don't know. I understand that people are sometimes born into situations that are not the best. Their childhood may have been bad. Things may have happened to dampen or even kill their spirits. People can be cruel and hurtful. Hopefully, if you are reading this book, you have a desire to have joy in your life. Know, please know, that no matter what you have gone through, you can determine to have joy in your life. It is there for you. No one else can give it to you. You have to choose joy for yourself. You can have self-pity, be broken- hearted over something, hate, and be unforgiving of yourself or of others, or you can choose joy and make the decision to think differently.

To think differently, you may have to completely change your mind, your very way of looking at things. Train your mind to go to joy rather than to sad or mad. Pay attention to where your mind goes in different circumstances. When someone cuts you off in traffic, honks their horn at you, etc., rather than go to anger, try blessing them. Say "bless you today," "peace be to you," "Lord, protect and bless them." In a situation at work when you feel yourself starting to get upset, stop, step back, breathe, and rethink your attitude. Go to the bathroom for time alone and consider your response. Think on joy rather than anger. Where do you really want to go with this situation? When you find yourself rattled and frustrated, back off and calm yourself. Think about the real importance of this, the long-term importance. Most things are not as important as we think they are at the time. Ten years from now, will this really make any difference? You can often see what is most important by this ten-year test. In the big scheme of things, ten years from now, will it matter?

Your health, your blood pressure, and stress levels—now they matter. How you react to a situation may have long-term, damaging effects on your health.

Learn to live and let go of much, because in reality, very few "things" matter. People matter, we matter, our health matters, and those we love matter. Decide what is important to you. It may take a while to sit quietly and evaluate what is in your life and why. We often get so busy with the everyday chores and things in our lives, we fail to see what is happening to us. We can start to lose our joy gradually, and before we even know what has happened, it is gone. We didn't even realize it has been taken. We have allowed "things" to steal our joy. These may even be good things, but not the best for this time. We must notice and pay attention to what is happening, and work to get our joy back.

What gives you joy? Is it the early morning sunrise, reading, writing, singing, running, biking, being with your family, or time alone? Whatever it is, work to get it back. Take time to be joyful every day, and guard your joy closely. Do not allow others to rob you of your joy. It is priceless and precious. It is your own joyfulness!

The more joy we give out, the more we receive back. I believe this with my whole heart. By loving and caring, we become more joyful inside. You can always give a smile and love to those around you—always. You can offer relief and light in this way to others' problems or hurts. You can choose to do this every day. By living this way, you will be joyful, as well as spreading joy to others. It is contagious, you know?

> "How far you go in life depends on your being tender with the young, compassionate with the aged, sympathetic with the striving, and tolerant of the weak and the strong. Because someday in life you will have been all of these."

- George Washington Carver

⊨⊧

CHAPTER 9

Who Will Cry At Your Funeral?

$\mathcal{I}$ read this question, "Who will cry at your funeral?" and it spoke to me. Who cares for you? Pay attention to these people. In life, we often take our family for granted or get so busy with life, just living day in and day out, we don't pay thought (not real consideration) to those we love. Who will be with you at the end of your life? Love the ones you love well. Pay interest in them. Care for them. Their love is precious. Treat it as such. Guard it carefully. People may disappoint you in life, and you may disappoint your loved ones, but forgive and love as best you can, always. People grow, they change, and we all think we are doing right and the best we can. Maybe you don't think someone is doing their best, but try not to judge them or be unforgiving. "Bend, don't break." Understand. "Walk a mile in their shoes," as the old saying goes. I am not saying this is easy. It is not. But use that theory of what does this "situation," "thing," "whatever" matter in the long run in the real scope of life? Most arguments, misunderstandings, etc. will work themselves out in time, if we will just lighten up.

In this same frame of thinking, what will people—and especially your loved ones—say about you, or think about you, when you are gone? What do you want them to say about you? I want those I love to say I loved them and tried to spread joy to them and others all my life. I want them to think I made a good difference in their lives. I want them to be proud of me. Then I ask myself, "What do I need to do differently to make this happen?" These are things to think on, right? Pay attention, and don't lose sight of your purpose. Life often gets in the way of everyday life. It takes our time and our thoughts. We must constantly pay attention and refocus on what's happening in our life, in our attitudes, and in our relationships. Watch your joy. Don't let it slip away through your busy day, your busy life.

Being aware of the gifts of life, the "*little gifts of joy*" we are given each and every day, and being thankful and appreciative of these gifts, is a path to open up more joy and blessings in our lives. Be aware, notice, and appreciate everything and everyone. Practice saying 'thank you' more often. Make yourself a blessing—a "*gift of joy*" to those who share your days.

> "What do we live for if not to make life less difficult for each other."
>
> - George Elliot

> "One day you will just be a memory to some people. Do your best to be a good one."
>
> - TryLife Quote

What words or memories do you want shared about you at your funeral? What do you want to leave as your legacy? If you go about each day as if it could be your last on this earth, you will choose more right, good things. You will help others, show more care and love, and think outside of only your own wants. This is a good way to live every day. I love the above quote from George Elliot about making life less difficult for others. This is a wonderful goal. Notice what you can do to make others have a less difficult life.

CHAPTER 10

Give The World A Smile & A Kind Word

"A kind word is like a spring day."

- Russian Proverb

Make it your practice to let only kind words come from your mouth. Think before you speak, and practice smiling as you talk. It is very difficult to be speaking unkind or angry words when you are smiling. Plus, a smile is an instant face lift! Remember that.

Norman Vincent Peale said, "Change your thoughts and you change your world." So if you want to have joy in your life, think on joy! It is really that simple. This doesn't mean we will never have bad or sad times, but we will be less likely to fall into a pit of depression and remain there. Seek joy, be around joyful people, read good, inspiring books and articles, listen to up-thinking speakers, and do fun, uplifting activities. Work at being joyful.

"Life is short and we have not too much time
for gladdening the hearts of those who are
traveling the dark way with us. Oh, be swift
to love! Make haste to be kind."

- Henri F. Amiel

Gladden someone's heart today as you travel throughout your
day. Chances are as you cheer their hearts, your own will be
lighter and happier. Be happy, be light, be joyous and fun! Why
not? What do you have to lose? Just frown lines.

Little things matter in our life. The "*little gifts of joy*" sprinkled throughout our days add so much to our life, if we aren't so
busy that we overlook them. This is why we must pay attention
to our ordinary days and times as we go through life one day at a
time, so we don't miss every little, small, joy-filled time. Watch
carefully for your "*little gifts of joy*," and your days will become
filled with them. At the end of your day, it will take an entire
page to write them down, and you will smile as you recall them.

"It is often the little things, the small revela-
tions that make a great deal of difference in
handling disappointment, frustration and
loss. They help us celebrate moments of joy by
enabling us to unearth the underlying goodness of things."

- Alexandra Stoddard

Whatever each day brings, make the best you can of it. Add a touch of joy to your day as you go along. Share joy with those around you. Being joy-filled adds beauty to your face. Look in the mirror. Smile. See how much better you look?

A smile and joyful attitude will help in <u>every</u> situation of your life. So put on a smile and go forward joyfully!

Make it your habit to speak only the good. While you are smiling, as you go along, you can also develop the habit or skill of speaking the good—finding the excellent rather than the fault. Then bring the positive you find to light. Tell others. Share it with others. Speak the good to others. This will catch on. You will be in demand because others will enjoy being around you. Always have a kind word to say. When you catch yourself saying something other than good, stop in mid-sentence and restart. When we encourage and say something helpful about others, it puts superior words out into the world. Discouraging words never help anyone—neither the one who says them, nor the one who hears them.

Make an effort to appreciate others. We all want to be valued. It is a need of human beings. When we get outside of ourselves, think of others and be grateful for them; it spreads joy to them and, in turn, to us. Pay attention to what others do so that you can brag on them. You can write them a note or say it out loud to them, but let them know that you noticed something they said or did. This will make them do even more good as they realize others noticed and esteemed them, and it will cause you to notice and show thanks more often. It is especially good to notice children and value, encourage, and uplift them.

This will help them thrive. We are often guilty of pointing out mistakes or negative qualities of children, but we do not make the same effort to point out their good qualities or successes. We should major on their good points, their strengths.

> "We're here to add light, not point at the darkness."

> - Alexandra Stoddard

I love this quote. How true. Often in this world, we get upset about how things are, and we talk and complain, fuss and fume to others. This helps no one. Usually it gets us more upset. We certainly don't seem to solve the issues this way. Why point at the darkness, add to the misery, and accentuate the negative? It isn't good for you or me. Instead add light. Think on the good that is happening. Dwell on this. I truly believe there are more good people in the world than bad. Most people want to do what is right, and are trying the best they can. We must encourage and uplift the good, add light, and bring their good deeds into the light.

If there were a news program that shared only good stories of fine things people had done, would people watch? I think they might. I know I am starved for good news and high-quality shows. If I am, surely others are. Each one of us can and should shed light in this world. Shine all around you. Don't point to darkness, but point to light. Point to the joy in life.

You can do this by sharing your joy with all to whom you come in contact. Smile as you go throughout your day. Speak with kindness to the checkout clerk at the store; bless others with a kind word; be thankful and grateful to the people who serve you and help you in restaurants and stores.

> "You must be a bit too kind in this world to be kind enough."

- Unknown

> "In your whole life melody the music is broken off here and there by rests, and we foolishly think we have come to the end of time. God sends a time of forced leisure, a time of sickness and disappointed plans, and makes a sudden pause in the hymn of our lives, and we lament that our voice must be silent and our part missing in the music whichever goes up to the ear of our Creator. Not without design does God write the music of our lives. Be it ours to learn the tune and not be dismayed at the rests. If we look up, God will beat the time for us."

- John Ruskin

Embrace your life. Live it joyously as long as you have a song in you. Make it what you want it to be. Be proactive. Be involved. Do not let it pass you by.

Make each day a day of joyful expectations. Instead of wishing for what you don't have, look with joy at the blessings you have and be grateful—always grateful. Attract good things into your life by thinking on good and doing good. Be a positive light in your world. Give your world a smile. You may be unable to change the whole world, but each of us can change our little part of the world for the better if we try.

Pay attention to your attitude, your smile, your words, and your actions. Totally enjoy life. If you don't like the way something is going, change it, or change your attitude about it, your response to it. Make a difference. Do something positive; don't just sit around and complain. Often a bad situation just takes some time. We may need to step back, step away, and give it some time. Rest your mind. A well-rested, quiet mind often brings clarity to a situation. Never rush in when you are tired and irritable. This causes more issues.

It is mainly our thinking that determines our attitude, not necessarily how things really are. Think about this statement. Do you need to change your thinking about a certain situation? Smile and go forward.

CHAPTER 11

Gratitude — Allow Things To Be

*P*ractice gratitude and delight rather than complaining and worrying. This will work much better for you.

Complaining and worrying never-never-never helps anyone or anything. Think, really think. Can you ever think of one time, one example, where complaining or worrying has ever helped anyone? I can't. These two things only destroy and hurt. So when you feel yourself complaining or worrying— stop it! I said stop it! Change your attitude, the way you are seeing things, the way you are thinking. Alter your response to the situation, and this will transform you for the better.

Don't sit around wringing your hands, worrying, obsessing, thinking or saying, "poor, poor pitiful me." Think up; think on joy. Adjust your thinking and revolutionize your ways. Keep beautiful, cheerful things around you. Read good books. Listen to wonderful music. Look at beautiful paintings. Do good for others. Love, live happy, and be filled with joy. What you dwell on is up to you!

> "Allow things to be as they are rather than pushing to make them conform to your agenda."

> - Candy Paull

O-o-oh, the above quote got me. This is difficult for me. I am very bossy by nature and like to be in control. My children, grandchildren, and those who know me will say "Amen" to this. I do know this is a good piece of advice—not to push for your own agenda. I have to work on this constantly. I like to make things happen and often push for my own agenda. I also know from experience that pushing to make things conform to my agenda isn't always a good thing because I don't know what is right for everyone else. Allow things and people to be as they are. It is their life, their decision to make. I used to tell my David, "Don't give your advice unless it is asked for." But then again, he didn't ask my advice or opinion on that, either. This is very hard to do when you have a bossy, take-charge personality like me. Oh well, I just have to keep working on myself—but not others. You can only change yourself, no one else.

> "Be kind, everyone you meet is fighting a hard battle."

> - John Watson

Be kind to yourself. We are often more unforgiving of our-selves than of anyone else. Be gentle, loving, and kind to your-self. Give yourself some slack—lighten up on yourself, laugh at yourself, and laugh often. Laughter is the best, greatest medicine! Allow things just "to be" sometimes. You are not in charge of "fixing things"! It is not up to you!

CHAPTER 12

Choices—We All Have Them

W̶e have choices always. We can choose to be unhappy and look at things in a negative light, or we can choose happiness and look up. It's all up to us.

> "We're swallowed up only when we are willing for it to happen."

> - Nathalie Sarraute

Reclaim your joyful life by your choice to do so. Others can only make you angry, sad, and miserable when you allow it. It is up to you to make the choice how you will respond to others.

I have seen—and I know you have, too—those who mope around, whine, cry, and complain all the time. When you ask them how they are, you immediately wish you had not asked. To them life is always hard, tough, rough, sad, or tragic. They expect bad and are not disappointed because their life is bad. What we expect we most often receive. If you are a bit guilty of feeling this way, you can change. Just determine to change your thinking. Your thinking is a habit, and habits can be broken. It's not always easy because we have programmed and trained our minds to think this way, but it can be done. Try it. When a negative thought comes to your mind, recognize it as negative and rethink it. Let nothing negative come from your mouth. Think on good. Think joy. Take joy. It is there in the world, all around you, if you will only look for it.

Thinking in a positive frame of mind does not mean that you will never see negative or bad things, but it does mean you won't dwell on them. Through personal experience, I have found that when we are looking for good and expecting it, it usually comes to us. There will always be good and bad in life. It is our job to major on the excellent. Look for it. Expect it. Be thankful for it. Enjoy it. When you look for it, it will be there. Good can come even out of the bad sometimes. There have been times in my life when I thought what was happening was awful, the worst thing ever. After I came through the situation, God turned the bad into wonderful for me. I could then look back and see how I had changed for the better because I went through this hard time.

Often problems in our lives are referred to as muscle builders, building us up into a stronger person. I have heard problems described as diamond polishers, knocking away the rough edges, helping us to shine and sparkle more.

> "Be strong and of good courage; be not
> afraid, neither be thou dismayed; for the

Lord thy God is with thee whithersoever thou goest."

- Joshua 1:9

Make the best of whatever comes your way. Look for the good—the joy—and you will find it.

"Nurture your mind with great thoughts for you will never go any higher than you think."

- Disraeli

"I have made some bad choices, I have made some so-so choices, and I have made some good choices. The most important aspect of them is that they are mine—all of them."

- Anne Wilson Schaef

Forgive yourself for your bad choices and move on. Let go of this and don't beat yourself up, but just learn from the mistake and don't repeat it. This is where growing older gets good. Hopefully, we have learned from our bad choices and grown wiser. I said, "hopefully!"

Iron, left in the rain
And fog and dew

With rust is covered——Pain
Rusts into beauty too.

- Mary Carolyn Davies

Somewhere I read the following statement: "A life without pain is a life of non-living." If you live, you will have pain; just know this. The success is to allow the pain to give you heart, to give you empathy, to make you into a more loving and understanding person——never to turn you into a bitter, defeated person. Grow into a more beautiful you by your choice to have joy, to major on the beauty and joy of life. Grow in love, grace, and joy!

We must learn to accept, to a certain extent, what happens, make the necessary adjustments to cope with the situation, and then move onward and upward. Life changes. It does not stand still. Flow with it. Change and grow with it, always going forward and becoming better as you learn more, go through more, and become more.

As we live, grow, and change throughout our lives, we realize we have completely transformed from who we once were. Our likes and dislikes have changed. Our wants and needs have altered. What we truly value has become different. Our joy has even evolved. We can find joy in new things and be more sensitive to joy. Life gets "sweeter as the days go by," it has been said. My joy has become deeper and fuller. My pain has also become deeper and fuller. One can have pain and still have joy. These may not seem to co-exist, but they do. External things aren't as important as they once were. This may come from the fact that as we live life, we come to understand what is true and important—real things, not false things.

Joy inside is a real, true joy. It is a joy that circumstances, problems, or sickness cannot destroy because it is our joy, bubbling up from a depth within, a place of peace, of love, and richness.

Hope. That is what brings joy. Hope, even in the depths of despair. A hope that there is life after death, a heaven for eternity, sunrise after the night, birdsong in the morning, a smile again, peace after the storm, love after rejection, laughter coming again. Always hope! Never give up your hope and joy! This will keep you going, keep you loving, keep you living and looking forward to another day—this thing called hope. Think on it. Read about it. Encourage yourself to have hope and joy always. Choose joy and hope!

CHAPTER 13

Hip-Hip-Parade

*E*xplode with joy and make your life worthwhile!

"You only live once—but if you work it right, once is enough."

- Joe E. Lewis

Live with effervescence! Make celebrations and ceremonies to enjoy every day. When she was little, my great-niece, Annie, made the mistake of saying "hip-hip-parade" instead of "hip-hip-hooray," and our family has taken this up as our saying when things are exciting. We say "Hip-Hip-Parade!" That's a great statement, isn't it? It is joyous and exactly correct.

You can celebrate each day if you want. Just find something to be excited about and then go for it. It may be the sunrise, the sunshine, a business decision, lunch with a friend or loved one, coming home in the afternoon, staying home all day, the beautiful sunset, the end of a trying time in your life. Anything can become your merriment. Live big. Hip-Hip-Parade! Make big deals out of your childrens' joys, your friends' joys. Just find joy and ways to rejoice everywhere you look. It makes life more fun. Have many "hip-hip-parade" moments. Watch for them. Notice them. They are all around you each day. Enjoy yourself every day! Make joy all around you. Scatter it like fairy dust. Fling it out everywhere!

> "Happiness is not a state to arrive at, but a manner of traveling."

> - Samuel Johnson

Be passionate about even the seemingly small things because there really are no small things. Everything is of importance. Do things with your special style and flair. You have your own style and flair, even if you don't yet know it. You can find your flair—your personality for doing things in a special way—if you pay attention. What are your favorite colors? What are your favorite foods? What do you enjoy doing? Pay attention, even down to the smallest things. What do you like? Notice how you prefer to do things, how you want to live daily, and make time for the things you enjoy. Drink coffee from the kind of cup that delights you, use the colors that make you happy in your napkins, use the kind of bath towels you desire—the color, the softness, the texture. Listen to music you enjoy. Music can set a mood of peace and calm or, on the other hand, excitement, joy, sadness, or blue, moody times. Pay close attention to the music to which you listen, and also to what you watch on television. Many people have their televisions on constantly when they are at home, even if they aren't watching. What is being said you hear, whether you realize it or not. And the news? Oh no! Sometimes watching this will depress you. When I found myself talking back to the TV news anchor, I realized it was time I stopped watching. Very seldom is TV news good news. You can learn of current events that are necessary to know in other ways. I had to stop watching the news for my own sanity and peace of mind. Notice if it is upsetting and depressing you. You may need to let it go for your better health and better self. TV can rob your joy. You have control over this. Turn it off, and be very selective as to what you listen to and watch. We may need to know about world and local issues (sometimes we may not), but be particular about how you get your news, how much you choose to hear, and the time of day best for you to read or hear this.

The people and information with which you surround yourself can either make you more joyful or kill your joy. Again I say, be very careful.

Keep yourself enthused and inspired with life. Do joyful things along with the mundane. You can make the ordinary enjoyable if you will use some imagination and creativity. Write your "to do" list on brightly colored note cards or index cards. I sometimes write with colored ink. Line your drawers with beautiful drawer liner, or for a less expensive way, use pretty wrapping paper. Then spray with perfume or place a pleasant-smelling bar of soap in the drawer. Make your office at home or work special, even if it is a cubical. Make a bulletin board pretty by covering it with fabric in keeping with the season. You can tack this on with push pins and change it out easily this way. What makes you joyful? Colors? Lots of light? Books? Quotes? Pictures? Find things that make you smile and happy, and then incorporate these things into your everyday life. I love flowers and try to keep them in my home. When I had an office away from home, there were always flowers on my desk. These do not have to be expensive. One daisy in a pretty vase will do. A tiny vase with a flower from my garden in the windowsill makes me smile. If you love it, have it around. Make joy happen wherever you are. You carry your spirit with you wherever you go. I love that in the Volkswagen Bug cars, they have installed a vase to hold a flower on the dashboard. Whoever came up with this idea is my kind of person.

You have an energy, a presence, a style, a flair; make it a joyful one!

Anything that delights us or makes us happy will help us. Choose wisely and help yourself. I have read that colors contribute to our mood. Color your world—joyful!

Yellow is the color of sunshine, the happiest color, and makes me optimistic and happy. A spot of yellow smiles at you and is welcoming. Yellow may be my favorite color.

Green calms me and brings peace into my world. It reminds me of spring and freshness. I love to put a green fern leaf into a vase by itself. This looks so fresh to me and helps me breathe deeply.

Blue is a peaceful color and meditative. It is a crisp, clean color and blends well with other colors.

Red is aggressive, full of fire and energy. Red is a strong, powerful color. I enjoy a spot of red or orange in a room. I especially love red toile or red checks mixed in a room. Red and orange are happy colors to me!

When you choose colors, notice what they mean to you and how they make you feel. Colors can make your world at home better. Color your world joyful!

Say "Hip-Hip-Parade," celebrate today, be excited, go!

⊨⊧

CHAPTER 14

Keep The Joy - A Childlike Heart

How do we keep the joy, the "wow" in our life? One way is to keep your childlike heart. Keep your curiosity alive and well. Be amazed. Be interested in new things. Never stop exploring, learning, changing, and growing. Pay attention to life. Love life, and it will love you in return. Ride the Ferris wheel, play in the snow, jump in rain puddles, have pillow fights, laugh out loud often. Never allow your joy to dry up and slowly die. Be spontaneous often. That sink of dishes can wait awhile. Play with the kids now. Make some mud pies or real cookies together. Enjoy the day. It is never too late to be a kid at heart!

> "The older you get, the more important it is not to act your age."
>
> - Ashleigh Brilliant

"Life was meant to be lived and curiosity must be kept alive. One must never, for whatever reason, turn his (her) back on life."

- Eleanor Roosevelt

"Life's under no obligation to give us what we expect."

- Margaret Mitchell

Often we allow our joy to be robbed from us because of our expectations, our thinking again. Always dream and plan, but don't expect. And don't allow yourself to become down and depressed because your expectations weren't met. How often we miss the good that is happening right now in our lives because we are so busy concentrating on something ahead. We actually have very little, if any, control over anything, except our thoughts and attitudes.

"Make the most of what comes and the least of what goes."

- Unknown

This is so true. If you are the type of personality that looks at the bad side of everything, then this is an area you really might want to work on. You can change your reaction if you retrain your mind. When you start to think in this old, negative way, notice it, stop, and rethink the situation. What is really important right now? Major on the joy, the good, and let the bad slip away.

There are people who have so much good in their lives, but won't allow themselves to be really happy. They look at what they don't have rather than at all the good they do have. They major on their lost expectations, not on the great joys they could have if they would only see. One of the most tragic things about this is they hurt their loved ones so much with this attitude. They miss much joy in their lives by being skeptical and seeing the glass as half empty rather than half full.

There have been times in my own life when I would be looking forward and planning something, and then finally arrive at my destination, enjoying everything. But then I would start thinking about how soon this would be over, there wasn't much more time, and thus cause myself to miss some of the joy and happiness of the moment by worrying about it soon being over. I allowed this by my own thinking. Now when I start to do this, I stop and change my thinking to realize I am enjoying, and will continue to enjoy, every minute fully.

Taste every drop of joy you can every day. Watch for it. Appreciate it. The joy of life is precious and wonderful.

> "This is the art of courage: to see things as
> they are and still believe that the victory lies
> not with those who avoid the bad, but with

those who taste, in living awareness, every drop of the good."

- Victoria Lincoln

Accept reality, but continue to see and experience the joy, the good in the world. I truly believe there is still much more good than bad. If this weren't true, then the good things would be making the news rather than the bad. Major on the good. Encourage yourself and those around you to do this.

As we grow older, we hopefully grow wiser. Don't allow your brain or your body to dry up. Continue to feed your mind with good thinking, and keep your body moving. Don't allow your light to become dim, dull, and less brilliant. Watch it burn brightly. Seek to remain young at heart. By keeping your joy alive, you can do this.

"Keep a young heart in your aging body."

- Wayne W. Dyer

"Refuse to let an old person move into your body."

- Wayne W. Dyer

I put my faith and trust in God, and this gives me a firm foundation in my life. Sometimes the road does get bumpy, but God sees me through. He is a solid and steady base. Life gets hard some days, and things may not be joyous, but have faith that God will give you joy again. Keep looking for the joy! Never lose that childlike heart. One of the things I loved most about my David was his childlike heart and spirit. He loved life and enjoyed it. Sometimes he infuriated me because he wouldn't grow up, and I would complain. But most of the time, he made me laugh because of his fun. We adults need to laugh more often and remember what it was like to be a child. We may need to act adult in some things but remain a child at heart in others.

CHAPTER 15

Focus On Joy

*I*f we spend too much time talking and thinking about our struggles, we will focus too much energy on them. The more you think and talk about a thing, the more magnified it becomes. So think on the solution, on the good that can come out of the struggle. Train your mind to go to the good. Keep the right perspective in a situation.

> "Be cheerful and the bearer of good news, no matter how minor."

> - Unknown

Shine your light on what is right. Focus on good things. As I have said before, "think up!"

> "People are like stained glass windows. They sparkle and shine when the sun is out, but when the darkness sets in their true beauty is revealed only if there is light from within."

> - Elizabeth Kubler Ross

Allow your light, your joy, to shine from within yourself. Smile. Lighten up the room. Be filled with wonder and awe every day. There are great things happening all around you. Don't worry about tomorrow and what might happen. Think on the good things that are happening now. Be aware of your light. Shine!

If you look for problems, you will find them. Look for good, and you will find good. Recognize the good in people and expect it. When you are faced with a problem, either pray and do what you can to change it, pray and walk away from it, or pray and allow and accept it. Accept the fact that you cannot fix everything, but know you do have a choice about your reaction and attitude toward everything that happens.

When we learn to allow ourselves to grow and change for the better through our problems, pains, and sorrows, we become the winner. Try to take things at ease as much as you can. Let a lot of "stuff" go. We may have to overlook a lot in our daily lives in order to enjoy our life. Our reaction and attitude can make all the difference between a great day and a bad day.

Be energetic, enthusiastic, spontaneous, and joyful. Get to know how to have fun in your daily life. Start now—this very moment—living joyfully. Determine to do this. You can if you want to. Yes, you can! Your joyfulness or sadness is completely and totally up to you. It is your choice. Choose wisely. Life is short. Smile and be joyful! Today is your "*gift of joy.*" Unwrap it. Celebrate it. Let's have a party! Hip-Hip-Parade!

Don't put off living joyfully until a better time. The best is here and now—right now. Feel amazement and wonder this very moment.

In the mornings as I am sitting, reading, writing, praying, and planning my day, I have a note card (brightly colored I might add) where I write my list of things to do. I always will either write in one fun thing to do that day, or leave a blank space for spontaneous fun things throughout the day. You should always do at least one fun thing every day, something you love to do: read a book you have wanted to read, go to a book store and browse through, buy a new magazine and look through it, go to the park, make a picnic lunch for two and take your husband or another loved one to lunch, work in your flower garden, call a dear friend, write a note to someone you love and appreciate, go out to lunch at your favorite restaurant, go for a walk, go for a ride and notice nature's beauty, go to the library, sit on the front porch swing, lay in the hammock and look at the sky, paint a picture. Think of something you love to do and then write it in. This makes every day fun and exciting. Never be so regimented that you leave out spontaneity. When someone calls and says, "Let's go to a movie," drop everything and just do it.

Focus on joy every day. Have fun in your life. You may have to work to earn a living, but you can still squeeze in some fun every day.

━≼┼┼≽━

CHAPTER 16

Change And Be Joyful About It

There is a Chinese saying, "Bend and be straight," that comes to my mind. We must learn to be flexible, to somewhat go with the flow of life. Remember: things that are rigid and inflexible often break. Adapt when change is necessary. For years, I hated change and fought against it. It frightened me. Now I see how foolish that was. Change happens whether we want it or not, so rather than fight it, learn to make it good for you.

> "The true wisdom is to be always seasonable, and to change with a good grace in changing circumstances."
>
> - Robert Louis Stevenson

You can look at change as an opportunity to start anew, to start fresh, and to have a new beginning.

"When water rushes toward a rock, it doesn't stop, but continues traveling around the obstruction. Things will never work out exactly the way you want them to. If you are rigid and cannot see fresh possibilities, you will be frustrated at every corner and detour. A rigid, inflexible branch of an oak tree snaps off in a hurricane."

- Alexandra Stoddard

Go with the flow. Accept some things, or change the things you wish to change, if you can. Embrace the change, and make the best you can of it.

There will be many surprises, changes, adventures, and new chapters in your life, if you live long enough. Be elastic and flexible. Flexible works and is much less painful than breaking.

"To exist is to change. To change is to mature. To mature is to go on creating oneself endlessly."

- Henri Bergson

New beginnings can be wondrously joyful times. They can be exciting, challenging, sometimes frightening, sometimes fun, fun! New beginnings—a turn in the road of life, new chapters in our lives. These are different ways of expressing change. We are afraid and unaccepting of it, aren't we? Why is this? We don't know what to expect, and if you are like me, I don't like that! It's different than what we have known. If we will alter our attitude toward change and look at it as a great new adventure, a new opportunity, it can be absolutely wonderful! It can be an exciting new time that draws us out of our ordinary days.

I read that we can transform ourselves by up to 50%. We cannot change anyone else more than 5%. Therefore, we only need to spend our energies working on ourselves. The other is a waste of our precious time. If someone you know has a bad character, in your opinion, it isn't your job to try and 'fix' them. You can only adjust your response to them, or walk away and leave them alone, whichever you choose. Try loving, encouraging, and praying for them. That is the best you can do for them.

Keep focusing on the good in your life. Count your blessings. Always be grateful. Remain calm during the storms and changes of life. They will pass. What goes on around you is not nearly as important as what goes on inside you. Find your peace, your joy, and your center. The more we are thankful and appreciative, the more joyfulness will come into our lives. Appreciate, give thanks, and be joyful, even for the changes.

CHAPTER 17

Forgive With Joy

One of the secrets to a life of joy is to live each chapter of our life as fully and as well as we possibly can, one day at a time. When that chapter is over, we can joyfully move on to the next adventure before us, knowing we did the best we knew how, never looking back with regrets and longing, but looking always forward to what's ahead. Look forward, with joy, to what is ahead and with joy to the very moment you are now experiencing. All you have is right now—this very important moment. Live it with joyfulness and thankfulness. Remember, regret is a waste of time. You can ask God for forgiveness, forgive yourself, and learn from any mistakes you feel you have made, but then move forward with joy and acceptance.

Life passes by. We must catch the joy, the excitement, and the goodness of this moment as it is lived, each day.

> "You have to accept whatever comes and the only important thing is that you meet it with courage and with the best that you have to give."

> - Eleanor Roosevelt

Find joy in the little or big things you do every day, but find the joy. Look for it. Search for it. It is there if we but look.

> "Let us then be up and doing with the heart for any fate; still achieving, still pursuing, learn to labor and to wait."
>
> - Henry Wadsworth Longfellow

> "The person who makes no mistakes does not usually make anything."
>
> - E. J. Phelps

It took me years to forgive myself for being a foolish teenager. Even in my adult life, I have times of making horrible mistakes and wrong choices. I finally forgave myself and others whom I felt had hurt me, or at least I am working to do this. Most all of us are young and foolish—or old and foolish—at some time in our life. Hopefully, we grew out of most of it, matured somewhat, and learned from life's lessons and from our errors. We must forgive ourselves and forgive others in order to find our joy. I am not perfect. You are not perfect. Let us forgive and live joyfully today. Today, as I go along, when I say something or do something that I feel is wrong, unloving, or unkind in some way, I try to stop immediately and ask God and myself for forgiveness. I say, "I'm sorry. That was wrong, unloving, or unkind."

Then I accept forgiveness and go forward, trying not to do this again. This practice leads to more joyful living. I often have to ask someone else's forgiveness, if I included some-one in my transgression or if I wronged someone by what I said or did. Keep forgiveness fresh. I don't always accom-plish this perfectly, but as I said, I am trying.

> "There is something infinitely healing in the repeated refrains of nature— the assurance that dawn comes after night, and spring after winter."

> - Rachael Carson

> "Into each life some rain must fall. Some days must be dark and dreary."

> - Henry Wadsworth Longfellow

Remember, rain brings forth flowers, and after dark and dreary days, sunshiny days will reappear. Be joyful and expect the sunshine to come again. Know that it will. And after a period of rain and gloom, we can appreciate the sunshine even more. This is the same in life. After a period of sadness, sickness, or heartache, there will be happy and joyful days again. We may even appreciate them more than we did before because we know how precious they really were. Without knowing pain, we cannot know real joy.

One way to keep joy alive in your life is to play. Laugh and play often. Think of fun things, joyful things, that make you laugh and smile. Then do them. En-joy!

Piousness—being holier than thou—has done more to hurt the name of Christianity than any other things, I believe. Be real. Be kind. Be loving. Be a good person to all whom you meet. It matters in life; it really does. Sometimes others cannot hear what you say because your actions contradict the words coming from your mouth.

If you mess up and are not kind sometimes, ask forgiveness. Shake it off; forgive yourself and do better from now forward. Do not beat yourself up over past mistakes. Be kind and loving of yourself as well as others. Learn and grow better from past failures. After all, it's not a failure if we learned something from it. One of my favorite sayings—and I don't remember who said it—is, "Regrets are an appalling waste of our time." I believe this with my whole heart. Regrets do not help us in any way. They can often keep us from moving forward. Instead, learn from your failures, and don't repeat them again. Forgive yourself. Ask for forgiveness if you have hurt someone other than just yourself, and then move on. Use this as a stepping stone, a path to better things—a new adventure, a new challenge, a new beginning!

Forgive yourself and others with joy in your heart, for when we harbor unforgiveness, we are the one who is hurt the most. Others may hurt you; pray for them and move on.

━╬╬━

CHAPTER 18

Everyone Remain Calm

avid, myself, and our neighbors, who are dear friends, had a saying. We would say this with a British accent, laughingly, "Everyone remain calm." We used this often in silly situations, but it is true in real life, serious situations as well. "Everyone remain calm."

Don't push yourself so hard. Sometimes back off, rest, and enjoy the day. Often we allow nonessential "things" to crowd out all our joy. We get upset too quickly and often unnecessarily. Remain calm. Breathe deeply. Smile and go forward. Go forward with joy.

Simplify and balance your life. Do not exasperate yourself. Let your hair blow in the wind; feel the breeze and the sunshine. Do not let nonessentials weigh you down. Let go and fly! Run barefoot through the grass. You're never too old to do this. So what if people see you and think you have lost your mind! They may see you having fun and decide to join you.

Our goal should be to have a joy-filled, well-lived life each day, to spread joy all around us, and to love those we love well. Don't sit and whine and cry. Get up and fling open the windows. Let the breeze blow fleshly in and surround you with sunshine and joy. Say aloud with me, "Hip-Hip-Parade!" Oh yes! Don't wait for something wonderful and exciting to happen. Make it happen! Go for it daily!

When you have problems remember, "What doesn't kill us makes us stronger."- Author unknown.

Sometimes it just takes time.

Make it one of your priorities to have joy and to share your joy with others. Make an effort. Go for the joy. Think joy. Believe in joy. Remain calm, but get excited, too. This may sound opposite, but you can be enthusiastic about things and yet remain calm in your inner spirit.

Rejoice in everything! Share good news. Get energized about everyday happenings. Pleasure is contagious. Look for ways to celebrate. You can if you want to. There may be problems or chaos all around you, but you can create an atmosphere of inner peace, joy, and calm. Watch out not to get upset just because those around you are upset. Remain in a calm place. Breathe deeply. Step away from the chaos and anger. Distance yourself from the stress. Think for yourself. Don't let anyone else control your emotions. "Everyone remain calm."

> "Let go of the people who cause constant pain;
> let go of the negativity that colors a room more
> darkly than any coat of paint. Keep close the
> people you love, the ones who stay engaged

and open to life, who bring joy and peace to
the house and garden."

- Dominique Browning

Let go of those with a poisonous spirit. Your spirit within you
can tell. When you are with someone, talking to them, and
something they say or do causes your spirit to react negatively,
take notice. Their personality may be poison to your spirit.

When we are in the flow of life, we want to sing, dance,
laugh, and reach out to others to join us in our joy. When others are negative and down in spirit, it will hinder our spirit.

Be cheerful. Make an effort for joy, and again I say, "Be
grateful and joyful!"

"Just living is not enough," said the butterfly.
"One must have sunshine, freedom and a little
flower."

- Hans Christian Anderson

Enjoy life. Smile and feel the sunshine. Go forth in freedom
and dance among the flowers. Learn to like whatever you do.
Do not allow your life to become dull.

"Let it be our happiness this day to add to
the happiness of those around us, to comfort

some sorrow, to relieve some want, to add some strength to our neighbor's virtue."

- William Ellery Channing

"Look around you and be distressed,
Look within you and be depressed,
Look to Jesus and be at rest."

- Anonymous

Be at peace (at rest) with yourself and with others. You can live in peace just as easily as you can live in chaos and with drama all the time. You choose by your attitude and reactions. Make it your choice to live peacefully, even in the midst of problems and struggles. Share your peace with others. Those around you will notice, and hopefully they will follow your example. You will learn when you are in a conflict, in a confrontation, or volatile situation, if you will keep your calm—your peace— you will come through it easier, and often your calmness will help calm those around you as well. "Everyone remain calm."

CHAPTER 19

Shaken — But Not Broken

*S*ome may say or think, "How can I think joy, be joyful, excited, and bubbly when there are those around me hurting, discouraged, facing problems, illness, and situations that are anything but joyful?" I have been writing and talking about an attitude of joy—a state of joy—even in the midst of problems. We may be surrounded by life's sorrows; however, we can find our center of joy, our attitude of thankfulness and gratitude, and our spirit of calm, peace, and joy and know that we will persevere. We can, and will, overcome the sorrow by our attitude and spirit.

I have said before that sometimes it is best to walk away from people and situations that are negative and constantly pulling us down. Sometimes these may be family members or loved ones from whom we cannot walk away. The situation may be one from which we cannot get away. In these instances, we need to learn how to deal with the person or situation in a different way and not allow our joy to be drained away.

What are some ways to do this, to react in such a way as to diffuse the negativity? Really look at how we have reacted or responded in the past, and if it isn't working, try to change our reactions. Rather than get frustrated, hurt, or angry, think positively and say words of encouragement and love—or possibly say nothing at all. Don't dwell on the things that bother you. Let it go. Change the conversation to something more uplifting. Can you find other things to talk about which are less upsetting to you? Possibly lead the conversation around to a subject more positive or less volatile. We may not always enjoy being around every member of our family, but we should not feel guilty because of this. We can always be at a place of peace if we choose. Try to find a common ground where we can relate in a positive frame of mind.

To some, this may seem the cowardly way out. But ask yourself, "Is the most important thing to have my say in this situation? Will it change anything really? Will it change their thinking? Probably not. Or is it more important to keep my peace and calm in myself and just let it go?" You are the one who must choose the correct response for you.

If you can voice your opinion in a calm and loving manner, maybe this is the right path for you. Choose your battles. Just know that some battles are worth fighting and many are not. I can recall knowing two brothers who were in their eighties and hadn't spoken in years—since their parents died—and they had fought over money and "things." Neither one of them would swallow his pride and ask for forgiveness or forgive the other himself. They died never having forgiven each other. Just think what they missed because of this—things that money could never buy or replace.

You may say, "Yes, but if I am always the one to forgive and give in, won't I be taken advantage of?" Possibly, yes. But you will live a life of fewer regrets. It is far better to be taken advantage of than to be the one who takes advantage of others. "It is better to give than to receive"—really! When we give with the right motive and spirit, we will receive peace and rest in our souls. Stubbornness, grudge-holding, and unforgiveness only hurt the ones who are harboring these attitudes.

There may be those people whom you just don't care to be around. Maybe they have hurt you or wronged you, and you have forgiven them and do not hold a grudge. However, you just don't enjoy their company, their personalities, their actions, or their attitudes. These people may drain your joy when you are around them. Sometimes you can stay away, but sometimes circumstances may require that you be around them. When you are in their presence, try to remain in a place of peace and calm, and keep control of your attitude. Keep it loving and as accepting as possible. They may be doing the best they can at the moment. We don't always know why people behave the way they do. If we knew their whole story, we might be more sympathetic to them. Try not to judge others or be critical. You can only change yourself, not others.

We don't have to put up with what we consider to be bad behavior from others. We can change our reaction or calmly walk away until we are in control of our own emotions. Think twice—possibly more than twice—before you speak or react to people who push your emotional buttons. You are in control of your own response. Remember this always.

How do we remain calm and joyful when our world seems to be caving in, things and people we have believed in have hurt us, disappointed us, and we feel totally upside down? I have had to rethink my entire value system, my life's way of thinking and believing. My foundation has been shaken, but not broken. During times like this, we must just keep on keeping on, put a smile on our face, and know that "this too shall pass." We will come through this, and life will continue on. If we but live through it, we will emerge a stronger person and be proud of ourselves for dealing with yet another of life's hard times. Listen to me: if you live long enough, hard times will come! They come to all of us. No one is exempt. Know that others have felt what you are feeling and have survived, and you can survive, too. The success is to survive with a joyous spirit and not turn into a bitter and defeated person. Your attitude, your spirit, is of great importance here.

Keep a smile on your lips, a spring in your step, and a song of thankfulness in your heart.

Life will go on, day will turn into night, and then another day will come. If you want to be in on life, just get up and start over again with a great spirit. Yes, you can live through this, whatever this is! Look for your joy in life, and love— always love—and be kind. If you face things with a loving spirit, then you are on the right path. This doesn't mean you have to just take everything people dish out to you and be beaten down. If you don't like the situation or the way someone is behaving, remember you can react to the person or circumstance differently, try to change the conditions, or alter your reaction or attitude towards the person or state of affairs. If you don't fight, there will be no fight!

When someone treats you bad, don't fight back with cruel, hurtful words or deeds. Keep yourself in a state of calm and peace. Breathe deeply and slowly; walk away until everyone can calm down. Often in a state of upset feelings, things can be said that can never be unsaid, and they may cause damage to you or others that can never be repaired. Before you speak in anger, breathe, step away, and think. Remain in control of yourself and your emotions. You can only be responsible for your words and deeds, no one else's. This is especially true in a family situation.

CHAPTER 20

Be Still In Joy

*W*hen we are overly tired and run down, things may seem worse to us than they are in reality. Be certain to get plenty of rest, try to eat right, and get exercise in times of stress. This will help you look at situations more positively. When you are tired and worn out, watch yourself so that you don't overreact to people and things. I feel this is why many young couples with children still at home have problems. There is so much going on in their lives. They are trying to work, keep their house running, take care of children, and are pulled in so many directions that they become fractious, unloving, and unkind to each other and often to their children. It is so difficult to find your calm center, your balance, when so much and so many people are pulling at you and demanding your attention, your time, your love, and little pieces of your life. It seems there is little left for you at the end of the day, or little left of you. You haven't even had time to think but are running on automatic pilot.

If you recognize this, then you can stop, breathe, and take charge of yourself again. Make moments of stillness in your day. Throughout your day, take mini-breaks where you are quiet; breath-marks for yourself. Close your eyes, breathe deeply, smell deeply, feel deeply. Calm yourself. Say a blessing to yourself. Thank God for something you see or feel, and then totally relax. Think joy. Put a smile on your face. It will make you feel better, I promise you. It really works. Try it. This is most important when things are crazy around you. Practice "taking joy" and a "mini-moment" of stillness.

When you feel you have come to the end of your rope and you've had all you can take, take a mini-moment of stillness and think on joy. Surround yourself with all the goodness you can possibly feel.

Today I lay on my hammock and looked at the blue, blue sky, bright apple green leaves on the trees overhead, and the white, puffy clouds. This was a moment of stillness and intense, pure joy for me. Try to make a habit of putting special moments of stillness and joy into every day. Giving "*little gifts of joy*" to yourself throughout your day is a blessing that will reap special benefits. The benefits may be to your health: reducing stress; to your mood and attitudes: uplifting your spirit; to your life in general: making the day an extra blessing to you. Take a little time for yourself today. Get away from the hectic, the loud, the rush, the madness and find your calm center of joy within. You can do this even if there is much going on around you.

Tune out. Switch off the noise and clatter. Breathe, relax, rest, and be still. Listen to the quiet. Feel your breathing. Rest and rejuvenate yourself. Smile. Laugh out loud about nothing. Life is dear and precious. Be thankful for the gift of life today.

Notice all your blessings. Pay attention to them. Don't take things or people for granted.

Even if you are in the midst of a crisis in your life, you can stop, breathe deeply, think on your blessings, say a little prayer of thanks, and then move on to handle whatever has been dealt you in a more positive light. Be thankful always, and be still.

CHAPTER 21

Joy-Filled Seasons

 W hen you have come to the end of something, you make a turn and then you are off on another road, a new beginning, a new adventure. Our lives are lived in chapters. Nothing in life remains the same. Just as there are seasons in the year, there are seasons or chapters in our lives. Live each one as fully, as passionately, as dearly as you can. Make the most of all that comes into your life, and then when it goes, let it go with grace and all the kindness you can.

We often have a difficult time letting go in times of change, but things come, and often go. We must grow and remake ourselves because if we don't, we are going to have a most difficult and painful life.

Nature will show us that change is a constant. Just watch nature, and you will learn how animals have to adapt to new situations.

There is no use to fight against it. You must learn to flow through your life. When things or people disappoint you, when they go away or alter their feelings toward you, go with the flow and learn to love and accept with grace. Be joyful and continue on along your road to see what wonderful things will come from this new bend in the road. This might be the most scenic road you have ever traveled. The bump you've just come through may have shaken you out of your rut.

I have often thought of the seasons in one's life as ages. There is springtime, when everything is fresh and new. Spring is birth to twenty, when life is young, and we are learning innovative things, experiencing feelings we have never had before, and growing. Then comes the season of summer—twenty-one to forty-five. Summer is a time of growing what we have sown in our springtime. Summer is fun. We usually decide on our work, we may start our families during this season, and we make a choice as to where we are going to have our home and begin to live our lives. Then autumn sets in around forty-six to seventy. We begin to reap our crops and get more serious about our life. This can be a fabulous time when we see the rewards of our labors. If we have children, they may be growing up, spreading their wings, and having families of their own. We see many of our dreams accomplished in this season of our life. It is often a season of great beauty. Then the season of winter, and I think of this as seventy-one until we are called to heaven. This season is a quiet, contemplative, and restful time. It can be a beautiful time. It can still be a very productive time in one's life. I have known many people in this age group who were productive, giving, loving, going, and doing and living vital lives, accomplishing their dreams.

"Forget your age and live your life."

- Norman Vincent Peale

"The older you get, the more important it is
not to act your age."

- Ashleigh Brilliant

You can get better as you grow older. You can be free to do
things you didn't take time to do when you were younger:
write a book, paint, take up photography, dance, sing,
garden—whatever you think you want to do. You can accomplish so much and have an even clearer vision of what you want
to do. Keep going and keep doing. Listen, be calm, and know
what it is you really want out of this life. Don't allow yourself
to think you can't because you are too young,   too old, too
busy, or too anything. You choose what you do with your time,
your energy, your brain.

"Life is what we make it—always has been—
always will be."

- Grandma Moses

"We should not let our fears hold us back from
pursuing our hopes."

- John F. Kennedy

With seasons of life—just as seasons in the year—there can
be great beauty and wondrous days, times of storms, and
cloudy, dreary days. But seasons come and they go, and life

moves on. If we will allow ourselves to enjoy the seasons and flow with them, life goes more smoothly. The seasons may be longer or shorter for some than the years I noted, of course. This was just my idea of the years broken down into seasons. But notice there is growth in all seasons, even winter. And there are wonderful, delightful, happy, joyous things happening in every season. The seasons in our lives can be fun, each one of them. They are different—a change—but fun and filled with "*little gifts of joy*." If we get stuck in one season all the time, life can become stagnant and boring. Differences and change can be lots of fun. We can see new things, do new things, and begin afresh. Just go for it—life! Love it and live it.

Think outside your little, narrow concept of what can be. People change as they go through the seasons of their lives. Hopefully, they become better, richer in spirit, more full of joy, and more giving and caring. Go with the flow of life through the seasons with happiness. Relish each season. Live it to its fullest potential. But when the season is past, go into the next season with hope and great anticipation of joy! Always look forward, not backward.

The past—good and bad—is over. Live your life today and make today the best you possibly can. Go forward with joy! Learn from the past and grow better and move on. Live your life well. Live as best you can without regrets, not second-guessing yourself. Do the best you can and then let it go! Move on! Let go!

Be strong and of good courage. Say, "I can do all things through Christ which strengthens me." Philippians 11:4

If we dwell on what was—wonderful or awful though it was—we can bring ourselves down in the present. My dad had a problem with this. The last twenty years or more of his life he couldn't enjoy for dwelling on the "good old days." While I loved to hear his stories of his boyhood and young adult life, he would not let it go and let himself enjoy what he had at the time. Nothing ever seemed to live up to what his mind had remembered as a "perfect time of life." It was terribly sad, really. He longed for these past days so much that it robbed his spirit of the present. He had so much spiritually to give to those around him.

> "With no looking back at what might have been, we are at peace."
>
> - Rose Fitzgerald Kennedy

We must move on, get over it, with no regrets! Forgive yourself and others, if need be, and look forward, with great anticipation, to what God has ahead for you, the great adventure!

Think on all the wonderful blessings you now have. Be thankful, appreciative, and joyful of your life, your season now—your life now! Live joyfully. Open your "*little gifts of joy*" daily. Be aware of them; don't look back to yesterday's joys to sustain you, but find new gifts of joy today, this very day.

Appreciate your yesterdays, your days of joy, and all God gave you, but always appreciate the now as well, and never lose sight of what blessings you have and will continue to have.

Celebrate! Hip-Hip-Parade! You are on to better things ahead, always moving forward with grace and joy into your new season.

CHAPTER 22

Complaint-Free Joyful Living

*I*n Will Bowen's book, *A Complaint Free World*, he admonished us to stop complaining and to become aware of how much we complain. He said, "If we change our focus, it will be easier to maintain a positive attitude." Also, he suggested turning your complaints into gratitude for the blessings you have. See the good instead of only seeing things to complain about. It is a great concept, and helped me to watch my words and hopefully stop complaining as often. He suggests that complaining affects our mood, and the words we speak out loud—such as "I'm tired, I'm worn out, I feel bad" and other negative comments—only make us live up to those words. They don't make anything easier. Complaining never helps anything. It usually only makes things worse or makes us feel worse. He challenges us to not complain or say anything negative for an entire day. It's hard, but it's a good challenge. The less you complain, the less you tend to worry.

Our words are very powerful. We need to think before we speak them. Will they be helpful words? Will they be kind, uplifting, encouraging words? Always make your words sweet, even to yourself.

One thing this complaint-free thinking has done for me is to assist me to let go of things over which I have no control, to accept things as they are, and better accept people as they are. I am a work in progress with this, but trying, and I can see it is a good thing. Any time we work on ourselves to do better, to be better, to improve in certain areas of our life, it's a good thing.

My Christian upbringing and Southern heritage have molded and shaped my thinking and beliefs. While I appreciate those who raised and taught me, I still must think things through for myself and question why I believe and think the way I do. One thing of which I am proud is that I was never taught to hate or to be disrespectful of anyone. Even when others thought and believed differently, my family taught us to love and respect them as human beings and to always be kind and loving to others. I appreciate my parents and grandparents for these values. The world has changed so much over the past sixty or more years, and values and acceptable behavior have become quite different. As one grows older, it is a challenge to see the differences and come to terms with them. You will have a true growth experience when you think through things you have always believed. You either reaffirm your beliefs, because you know why you believe them and have accepted these things for yourself, or you will make changes in yourself and your beliefs. This makes one a stronger, better person. If we just always accept what others have told us and what others say—never questioning why we believe a certain way—we may become weak and not have a strong foundation when the storms of life come. I continue to learn, question, and hopefully grow, and hope I will until the day I pass from this world into heaven.

> "Our outer worlds are a projection of our inner worlds."

- Will Bowen

> "Why do you look at the speck of sawdust in your brother's eye and pay no attention to the plank in your own eye?"

- Matthew 7:3

> "Love is unconditional acceptance and looking for the good."

- Dr. Denis Waitley

> "You have a choice with the words you use to create the life you live."

- Will Bowen

We must be wise in the choice of our words, thoughts, and actions. Here again I say "think joy" and become joyful. It can only do you good, and will do good for those around you. When we have a choice—and we do—why would we ever choose sadness, gloom, or hate?

Do not complain and focus on what you don't have, but look with gratitude at what you do have. Feel blessed always, and then seek to be a blessing to those around you. Share your joy with others.

Choose joy!

The world is in great need of joy. Each of us needs more joy in our lives, joy that is real; not this fake joy that we often think money and things will bring. Real joy will sustain us and last even through difficult times. A spirit of joy will shine through the darkness and bring us out on the other side. Joy will keep us fresh and new in spirit. Joy will bring others to us. People want to be around joyful, happy people. Joy is shining. It is light. It is exciting. It is soft and pure. It is wondrous. It is loving and kind. You can take joy, think joy, and be filled with joy if you want. It's all in your thinking. You can change your world. When doubt starts to creep in, think joy! When anger, hate, or unforgiveness start to come, think joy! When negative thoughts start racing into your brain, think joy! Get up and start doing good for yourself and for others and think joy! You can retrain your mind to think on joy rather than sorrows, hate, and unforgiveness if you choose to do so. It's up to you every day. How do you choose to live your life? Joyfully, I hope. It is so much healthier and happier than the other choice.

Oh, you may slip sometimes, but that's the good part. You can always forgive yourself and start again. Remember:

"The only difference between success and failure is that success gets up one more time."

- Unknown

Negative attitudes and negative thinking are difficult habits to break. To retrain one's mind to think differently is no easy task. Just keep on trying. Keep on working at this. Notice when your thoughts or words go toward negative comments or complaining, either to yourself or out loud. Stop yourself in midsentence, if necessary, and change that thought or statement. Is it going to help or encourage you or anyone else if you think it or say it aloud? If it's negative, it will never help! NEVER!! So either don't say it aloud, or change it before it comes out of your mouth. Parents and spouses, this is especially important for us to know and practice. Practice joyful responses often. Encourage, love, and uplift with your comments, both to yourself and others. Remember to be kind to yourself as well as to those around you. Do not complain and gripe! Stop it now!

CHAPTER 23

Joy – Not Gloom

D o not allow gloom to get inside you.

"The gloom of the world is but a shadow; behind it, yet within our reach is joy. Take joy."

- Fra Giovanci

There will always be gloom, problems, and sorrows in this world, but we must major on the joy and lift ourselves and those around us above the gloom. Always know on cloudy days, beyond the clouds there is sunshine. And in our lives, likewise, there is sunshine beyond the shadows. After problems, joy can be found again. Life can be rich, full of joy, and rewarding once again. Keep this knowledge in your heart, and pass through the valley as peacefully as possible, being aware and expecting sunshine and joy again. Never allow the gloom to get inside you. You have control over what gets inside you by your thoughts, choices, attitudes, and actions. Stay focused on what's real and what's important to you.

Sometimes one can began to almost feel guilty because your life is so full of joy, while others around you appear to be swallowed up in sadness or always seem to have negative feelings and thoughts. I truly believe that often—not always—but often we bring bad things on ourselves by our negative and down thinking and actions. Try thinking up and positive with a new attitude of joy, and see if good things don't happen more often. They will. If things aren't going right, change your attitude, change your spirit. Lighten your load. Try not to feel guilty when good things are happening to you. You would be happy and rejoice with others if good was coming to them, wouldn't you? Yes, you should always rejoice with others when good happens. So celebrate your joy, and make merry with others who have joy. Just have fun and live happily day-to-day.

"You can only be happy on a day-to-day basis." I read this somewhere and believe it to be so true. Be happy that you are filled with joy today. If others aren't, I really wish they would be. It is their decision; neither you nor I are responsible. You can only make yourself joyful. You can only love and encourage others as best you can. It is up to them to get on the joyful wagon. Oh, how I wish everyone could find their joy. I see people who are so bitter, so grumpy, and unjoyful, and I think of all they are missing in life—all the love, the beauty, the goodness of others. But they won't allow this into their lives. They have built their own wall around themselves, a wall where joy cannot get through or come over.

We build walls around ourselves for many reasons. Sometimes we do this so we won't be hurt, but this really doesn't help in the long run. We must learn to let go of our idea of control, our perfectionism, our preconceived ideas. Lighten up and just enjoy others and our lives as they are. Let the walls fall down. Let your troubles roll away. Life is just too short to live it with regrets and up-tightness. Lighten up on others, too. We don't know their hearts and what they have been through. We can only love and care about them and be joyful to them as best we can.

CHAPTER 24

Home — A Place Of Joy

We can make our homes a place of joy and refuge from the stressful world outside. This is the only place over which we have control.

> "Our home is modest but harmonious, quite simple, nothing extravagant, nothing for connoisseurs. But good for people and solid work."
>
> - Carl Larrson

The above quote describes my little cottage. It is a place of love, peace, and comfort from the storms of life. I feel safe and secure here and have finally found my home. I have lived longer in this cottage than anywhere else in my entire life; I love my charming, little Main Street Cottage. One of the reasons I love it so is because David and I renovated the 1890s cottage together. It was our home together, and we were happy here!

For years I worked as a realtor, and in those years I saw all kinds of houses. I have seen houses that were cold and shallow, as well as houses that were true homes, filled with love and laughter. The difference depends on the people who live inside. A home's atmosphere, whether a grand house or small, depends on those who reside inside and their attitudes. I truly believe a house—the building itself—reflects the attitudes of its residents. When people walk into your house, what do they feel? Hopefully, they feel warmth, love, and welcome.

Our family and friends have to be our priority, not things or possessions. We must keep ourselves real, keep our reality in check. A large house does not show success, but rather who lives inside the house and what love lives there. If we share our success and love with others, this is good. There is nothing wrong with having wealth, a grand home, and beautiful things as long as these are not our god and what defines us. There is an art to living well. The art is to take what we are given and make the most good out of it. Take care of your heart, your soul, and your life. Pay attention to the seconds, the minutes, the hours, the days, the weeks, the months, and the years as they go by. This is your life. Live it well! Live exuberantly. Live with effervescence. Create contagious joy!

> "If your daily life is poor do not blame it, blame yourself, for you aren't poet enough to call forth its riches."

> - Rainer Marie Rilke

Call forth the richness of this day, this time in your life. It is the best time of your life. It is what you have right now. Make the most of it!

Your home reflects your personality, your taste, your likes, and dislikes. Make your home a place of peace—a refuge for you, your family, and friends. What do you love? Have these things around you. Neatness, cleanliness, and order bring more peace and calm to your life. Clutter and disarray may cause you to be nervous and unsettled. If your home is untidy and it is overwhelming for you, just start out by taking one small area at a time and begin. Get boxes, label them, and store things out of season. Or get large trash bags and throw away what you no longer want or need. Better yet, for things that are still useful, but you no longer have use for, donate them to a church, center, or local charity. A good rule of thumb is if you haven't worn an item of clothing in a year—get rid of it! I heard this good piece of advice: when you buy something new, find something you have not worn in a year and give it away to keep your closet from becoming out of control. Declutter, get organized, neaten up; these things will help you feel more in control of your life. Then you can enjoy your life more fully.

Do not allow this to overwhelm you. Work on it one room, one closet, or one drawer at a time. Little by little you will feel more relaxed and sense you are accomplishing something good. A friend might help you. You could say "help me organize my closets, and I will help you with yours." If you can afford it, there are professionals who can clean and organize for you. If you hate this job, then work and do something you would rather do to make extra money and hire someone else to do your closet cleaning. But there is nothing nicer to see than an organized closet, drawer, or cabinet, and you will feel a sense of accomplishment afterwards. This brings me joy, but I am horrible about keeping closets and drawers organized and straight. I seem to be able to keep my house semi-straight and neat, but behind the closed cabinet or closet doors, things are often out of order. And this will bother me until one day it will reach its peak, and I will realize this is stealing my joy. I feel unsettled, like everything is a mess and out of control. I will have to buckle down and fix it—one drawer at a time.

When I tackle this project, it will make me feel great after it is accomplished. At first, it is almost overwhelming to me. But then I will start one room at a time, one section at a time, empty a drawer or cabinet, clean the empty drawer, throw away or give away what I no longer use, put down pretty drawer liner, spray with Febreze or a perfumed spray (depending on kitchen or bedroom), and refill carefully with much less "stuff." Then I will look at what I have accomplished and sit down with a glass of iced tea and "celebrate," making a joyful moment out of this.

In reality, the largest part of our joy is found at home. If your home life is poor, work on this. Love up your home. Pay special attention to the people who are there. We tend to be less attentive to our loved ones than those with whom we work or are casually acquainted. This is probably because we think they (our loved ones) are going to love and accept us no matter what, and we can truly be ourselves with them. But we should be our best selves at home and with our loved ones and think of their feelings, their wants, and needs. Work to create a loving environment in your home. It should be a place of peace and a refuge—a place you love when you come home. Make it as clean and pretty as possible. Have it smelling good, and have items around that you and others enjoy. Make your home fun for yourself and your loved ones. Love up your home, and love and live there happily!

Be extra attentive to your attitude at home. Make an effort to be loving and kind in all you say and do in your home. When you are in a bad mood, stay away from the people you love, as best you can, until you get control of yourself and can be happy and pleasant again. Tell them you are not in very good spirits and to please excuse you for a while.

Ladies, attitude problems and mood swings can come on us quickly. In middle age, we may be faced with menopause and have emotional upheaval. There is nothing wrong with asking your doctor for something to help you during times of chemical imbalance or medical issues, but do not allow yourself to use medical problems as an excuse to behave badly. I have known women who are out of control emotionally it seems, but then they can control themselves with other people when they want. It appears they are using menopause as an excuse to let their emotions and tempers go around their family.

I, myself, usually know when I am in a disagreeable mood and am acting badly. I try to stop and ask forgiveness from those to whom I am venting and then begin again. We sometimes let ourselves go more freely with our spouses and children because we are with them more than anyone else. These are the very ones we should be the nicest to. Do not let yourself become emotionally angry or agitated. Watch yourself and stop it. As Barney from *The Andy Griffith Show* would say, "Nip it in the bud." We—at least most of the time—know when we are in a bad mood, have a temper, or are being irritable. If we know it and pay attention, we can stop most of these unhealthy attitudes.

No one wants to be around a mad, fussy person, and you won't even like yourself if you allow yourself to become that person.

CHAPTER 25

Nurture And Nourish

A person can be happy and filled with joy if they choose to be. Light your own fire. You are alive today. You have the choice to go for it or not. Celebrate today! Be open to the joy and make opportunities for yourself. Change your attitude and change your life.

"When you sow love, joy grows."

- German Proverb

"Listen. Think first of someone else. Laugh a little. Gladden the heart of another human being. Take pleasure in the beauty and wonder of the earth. Speak your love. Speak it still once again."

- Unknown

> There is a Japanese saying that goes, "One
> kind word can warm three winter months."

Try to find a kind word for everyone. We are often quick to
criticize, complain, gripe, and fuss, but very slow to say kind
words. Say words of encouragement, words of praise, words
of recognition, and uplift someone every day. Compliment
someone about something. Look for ways to show approval or
encourage others. Every morning, before you leave your door,
make a pact with yourself that you are going to encourage and
uplift several people this day. Then do it!

Choose to live in the sunshine today, and let the shadows
and the clouds pass you by. Be at peace with yourself and others
as best you can. I love the slow, leisurely days of summer. Since
I was a child, and school let out for summer vacation, I have
loved these months and always looked forward to them with
great anticipation. I think, "What fun summer things can we
do: eat watermelon, go to the pool, go to the lake, catch light-
ning bugs, shoot fireworks, watch a parade, lie in the hammock
and watch the clouds roll by, pick lots of flowers, eat fresh corn
on the cob and other fresh garden vegetables and fruits, swing,
sit on the porch, grill out, or make homemade ice cream?" On
and on my list goes. Oh, summertime is a grand, fun time if
we will choose to live in the sunshine and enjoy the flow of the
season. Don't allow yourself to grow up. Keep that childlike
spirit and "play" often—every chance you get. Life is short.
Enjoy your summers. Two of my most favorite things are blowing soap bubbles and playing in the water sprinkler. These are

some ways to nurture and nourish yourself. You may not have the summer off from your job, but you will have days off, plus the daylight hours are longer in the summer. Usually people take a week or more of vacation in the summer. Enjoy the time you have. Plan for fun, and expect fun and joy. We usually get exactly what we expect and plan for. Lighten up and be a kid again with your kids, grandkids, or just by yourself. Remember how you felt as a kid on the last day of school? Remember how you thought the world was yours for the summer, and you had all the time in the world? Try and find that feeling of freedom once again. Let yourself soar.

You may have to find children to play with you to keep up the appearance of sanity. I have found one of the joys of being a grandparent is that we can play again with the kids, and no one thinks you're crazy. If they think this, it doesn't matter anyway. Play in the sprinkler today! Enjoy!

When you play with your kids or grandkids, you are making great memories for them. If you don't have kids or grandkids, you can adopt a friend's or neighbor's child—someone special whom you love. So many families live far away from their grandparents, and children could probably benefit greatly by having an adopted grandparent, aunt, or uncle. Reach out to others, and you will bless them and yourself at the same time. Watch for opportunities to bless others. They are there if you will notice. Just being thoughtful of others is such a *"gift of joy."* Kindness, thoughtfulness, caring acts—these all work to make our lives and the lives of others better. This ripple continues on and on to everyone we meet. It is as simple as "do good." Think and do good for others. Smile, love, and share always. This is not difficult. It gets easier and easier as we go along.

Nurture and nourish others and yourself!

> "We can't change the universe but we can nurture and nourish those near us. When we do all we can and bring forth our best, we are doing our share to make the world a more humane place."

> - Alexandra Stoddard

What can you do to nurture and nourish others? Watch for ways to be of help. There are so many things you can do if you will open your ears, your eyes, and your heart. People who have the talent for cooking can take a meal or a great dessert to someone who has been feeling under the weather, has company coming, or has just been low in their spirit. People who have the gift of encouragement can write a note. People seldom receive notes or letters anymore. These are always appreciated. You might take flowers just to cheer them up. If you are an artist, paint them a picture. Whatever you can do, use it to nurture and nourish others. Give of your time and talents. Maybe you can offer to babysit or help clean their house. Just do whatever you can to help others. When you try, you will be astonished at the joy you can bring into lives—and your life—at the same time. Everything good we do affects us in a positive way.

When we bring joy to others, it spills over to us. Giving "*little gifts of joy*" brings more joy into our own world. Giving and sharing is always a good thing. You may think you have no talent, but if you will look closely, you will find that you do. You just may not have developed your talent as of yet. Get out of yourself and do for others: those around you, your family, and then your friends. Then go on to others you see. This will grow and grow. Give, nurture, nourish, and be joyful in your spirit. There is always room to love and care, and there is always someone who needs our love and care.

If you ever have trouble with depression, the above is the greatest cure. Stop thinking of yourself, and get up and do something for another. It will work!

"Inaction saps the vigor of the mind."

- Leonardo da Vinci

When you just sit around without a purpose, with no goals in mind, you become tired and worn out. Inaction is the death of joy. Get up and get going. As long as you are alive, keep moving and keep doing.

This is different than times of quiet and solitude when you are reading, writing, praying, meditating, and having good times by yourself. These times of solitude are good for you. I am talking here of inactively sitting and becoming dull, down, and discouraged. We need to get ourselves "up and at 'em!" Becoming sluggish and stagnant is a "no joy status." Get your bootie up and get yourself going. Proper eating, sleeping, and exercise play a major role in how we feel. We have to watch ourselves here and pay attention to our body. Our body will tell us something is wrong if we will pay attention. If you are tired, rest. You may crave a good meal; have one. Moderation in all things is the healthy way. Go for a brisk walk. Get outside and breathe deeply. Believe in yourself.

"Attitudes are more important than facts."

- Karl Menninger

We have all heard the saying, "If you think you can, you can. And if you think you can't, you can't." This is so true. It has been proven over and over again that people can overcome major difficulties, handicaps, and problems by how their minds think. Get your thinking right. Read good books, listen to good speakers, surround yourself with people who encourage and inspire you. Take control of your own thinking. You have the ability to turn off, put down, or get away from voices that drag you down, sap your creative energy, and depress you. Take control of your own thoughts. This does not mean not to question yourself as to why you believe as you do, why you act and react the way you do. You may need to question, change, grow, and rethink things. This means anything that drags you down constantly in spirit and in love causing unrest, hate, unforgiveness, and bitterness is not good for your spirit. Let these go.

You may have been around people before who were critical, unloving, bitter, or gossips and when you left them, you felt bad because you had participated in these attitudes or actions. Just learn from this experience, and the next time you find yourself in a situation like this, be ready; recognize this and change your reaction. You may just step away, or you may try to say something good or positive to change the conversation. Whatever it takes, get yourself out of this downfall. It is within your power! Breathe, relax, and think before you speak. Leave with grace. Always try to remain in a loving place. Do not be critical of others, even if you disagree with them. People think differently. People are diverse. We have been raised distinctively. We have gone through various trials and life situations that have molded our personalities and helped to make us who we are. You know that saying about "walking a mile in their shoes"? So we don't judge them, but we can choose not to participate in their negativity.

> "Between the house and the store there are little pockets of happiness. A bird, a garden, a friend's greeting, a child's smile, a cat in the sunshine needing a stroke. Recognize them or ignore them. It's always up to you."

- Pam Brown

I love the statement "little pockets of happiness." It is very similar to my words, "*little gifts of joy*." So my idea is nothing new,

I suppose. I just read the above quote for the first time today, but it had been written before my "*little gifts of joy*" concept. I suppose it is true, "there is nothing new under the sun." But maybe if we say it, hear it, or write it in enough ways, the meaning will get through our heads and into our hearts. Notice the "*little gifts of joy*" God places in your life each and every day. Notice—see them and allow them to nourish and uplift you.

CHAPTER 26

The Sermon Of Your Life

As I was writing this week, I received a call that a dear friend's husband had died suddenly. We were all shocked because this was so unexpected. After the days of being with her and the family through the planning of the funeral, the funeral, and all that goes with this, when I finally sat down and reflected, I was brought to terms, once again, with how quickly life can be taken from each of us. There is no guarantee of tomorrow, next week, or next year. Right now, this tiny moment is what we have—all we have. We can get almost in a panic over this, or we can use this knowledge to live while we have life. When someone you know dies, it wakes you up to life and causes you to really see again what is important. The little, common, everyday things are the significant things. What you see, who you love, what you think, with whom you spend your time, what you spend your time doing . . . these are your life.

Make certain you reevaluate and prioritize the people and things who matter to you. You can easily get caught up in things that aren't crucial to you and let people who are not that central take up all your precious minutes, hours, days, and years.

You, and you only, have control over this. You choose how you spend your time and with whom. I know most of us have to work and earn a living, but I'm talking about those other hours as well. Often we let television, the Internet, or people who are not that key in our lives to take our extra hours, unaware as these hours just slip by unnoticed. We need to notice, or our time on earth will be stolen from us as busyness takes them.

It is good to take a close look at yourself and your time. I have heard it said, "Live each day as if it would be your last and also as if you would live forever." That is a difficult feat to accomplish. For me, I think it means notice, love, and appreciate others and the "*little gifts of joy*" sprinkled in your life. Be aware. Be grateful. Value the time that God gives you. Do your best to use it wisely. Be gentle. Be kind. Be loving. Have as much grace as you can. Try to do right. As I sat at my friend's husband's funeral, I thought, "What will be said about me at my funeral?" I read that we preach our own funeral with our life. This is so true. How we live day in and day out is the sermon of our life. I pray mine will be a good one!

> Yesterday is gone.
> Tomorrow has not yet come.
> We have only today.
> Let us begin.

- Mother Teresa

Go forward joyously and do the best you can. Make your life a blessing to yourself and to others. Say a kind word. Be an encourager. Smile at everyone you meet. Be calm and at peace with yourself and with the world. Think tranquilly. Act unruffled. If you take things relaxed and slowly, life flows more smoothly. It is when we become spastic and overreact that things get out of hand.

Remember, with God's help, you can handle anything! This is a major life lesson. It is absolutely true. Breathe, relax, pray, and then go forward calmly and confidently.

"Life is fragile—handle with great care." Care about how you react and respond to everyday life. Appreciate your wonderful life. Be thankful and in awe of the gift you have been given—the gift of another glorious day. You can make your day what you will by your attitude, your acceptance, your love, your joy, and your exuberance.

CHAPTER 27

Joy—A Top Life Priority

As I have been writing this book, I have continued to think of ways to put more joy into one's day, "*little gifts of joy*" to give ourselves each day. The main way to do this, I believe, is simple—just determine to do it. Making joy one of the top priorities in life is a great goal. To be joyful as we go about our day is a determination, a quest that we set out to accomplish. To have and give out joy is a great gift, a success in life. Life is filled with so many "*little gifts of joy*" when we are looking for them. This morning, as I was writing, I decided to sit outside on my patio. There was a nice breeze blowing, the sun was shining, birds were singing, the water fountain was gurgling, the nearby church bells rang out the hour, and then a beautiful hymn played. It was all such a blessing, and I stopped to notice and appreciate every moment. I kept seeing things that needed (I thought) to be done, but I sat still and reminded myself of my goal and made a choice to spend some joy-filled, peaceful time sitting, writing, and thinking. Things in life often distract us. These are sometimes good things, but they may not be the best thing for us at the time.

One of my friends is battling high blood pressure right now. It seems to me—looking on from the outside—that he needs to slow down and calm his worry and pace. This is simple, right? But then I do not know his inner thoughts or the pressures put on him by himself and the world. Only we can stop our own crazy thinking and destructive actions to ourselves. Sometimes we cause destruction to ourselves by the way we think and the way we choose to live. I do understand if you have children, a family, and people who depend on you for their livelihood and means, it is difficult to say, "I am going to slow down my pace and stop worrying, working so hard, etc." But if you kill yourself with an illness brought on by stress, worry, and overwork, this isn't going to help the family, is it? When we worry, fret, and overwork, we are not contributing to the real happiness of our family because we are uptight and stressed.

We appear to have a generation of abundance in things, but not in love and real joy. We need to possibly rethink our priorities. This is difficult to do when others around us have all the "fun toys" or all the "opportunities" we have been programmed to believe we must have to be successful.

We need to stop, breathe, relax, think of what real success means to us, and redefine our own philosophy. Have we bought into a false philosophy of success, of life? Have we allowed our faith, our hopes, and dreams to be stolen from us? How did this happen? It is never, never too late! I'll say this again; it is never, never too late! Well, maybe on our deathbed, but not until then—so start now!

Be realistic in some ways, but know that you can change your thinking. You can think on good, on joy, rather than the bad, the ugly, and the negative. You can turn the bad into good again if you want. Ask God to help you help yourself.

"Bacteria and other microorganisms find it easier to infect people who worry and fret," according to Dr. Leo Rangell. We hear that stress brings on numerous illnesses or, at the very least, contributes to them.

How can we stop worrying, fretting, and having stress and anxiety? Change our thoughts, adjust our actions and responses, and take joy instead. Think on joy. Think up. Look up! We have to lift our thoughts, our attitudes and rise above the problems. Think in a different way about our problems. Turn them over to God and work in a new way to solve them. Often we bring our problems on ourselves by our own actions, our choices, our attitudes. Rethink the way we have been handling the things we are worried about.

When I find myself down and discouraged for any reason, I have found the words from the song, "Count Your Blessings" works for me. I take a pad of paper and begin writing down every thing and every one who blesses me. I read somewhere a suggestion that you not stop until you write at least 100 blessings. When you practice this little "exercise of joy," you will be feeling much better. After this, get up and do something to be a blessing to someone else. Share yourself. Share your time. Get out of yourself. Write a note of appreciation to someone on your blessing list, telling them how much they mean to you and how they have blessed your life. Not only does this uplift someone and make their day more joyful—because this note will be one of their *"little gifts of joy"*—it will also help you. You will feel lighter, happier, and no longer discouraged. Why? Because you have given of yourself to someone else.

CHAPTER 28

Getting The Life Knocked Out Of You

"One thing after another happening to you can literally "knock the life out of you." The expression is realistic; life is knocked out of you, for a fact. Blow after blow can leave you pretty limp and discouraged. Ultimately you may feel so beaten that you crawl through life instead of standing up courageously and masterfully taking things as they come and handling them with sure skill and force. There is no fun in life for the crawler-through-life. The licked are always unhappy. But those who know in their hearts that they are equal to every challenge, minor or major, are the ones who get a huge amount of fun out of life."

- Norman Vincent Peale

*T*ry not to allow problems to run together and over-whelm you. Keep a "one-thing-at-a-time" attitude. Do what you can and pray. That is all you can do. Then smile and go forward. You can control your attitude. Do not get out of control. Think up, good thoughts; love and stay in a state of grace. Always love and be gracious.

When you keep this attitude of love and graciousness, you can come through feeling that you have handled the situation well and be proud of yourself. I read the statement somewhere, "You are as happy as you want to be." Know that sorrows, great sorrows, and disappointments come in life and often shake us to our very core. I also have read over and over of people with awful problems and tragedies who have overcome and lived through these and came out with amazing spirits—loving others and helping others through—all because of what they had been through themselves.

Problems, hurts, disappointments, and sorrows can make us stronger and more loving and understanding if we will allow this. "We can become bitter or we can become better" because of what has happened in our lives. Let us choose to become better! Love and be gracious always. It isn't always easy—and sometimes we may fail at this—but we can always ask for forgiveness and forgive ourselves for our failures and go forward again in love.

William Lyon Phelps said, "The happiest person is he who thinks the most interesting thoughts."

Marcus Aurelius Antonius said, "No man is happy who does not think himself so." So think yourself happy. Think joy, and then scatter that joy on to others. You have the ability to do this if you choose. Look for happiness every day. Look for those *"little gifts of joy."* Give *"little gifts of joy"* to others who come into your life every day. Expect to receive a gift of joy each day, and make it one of your main goals to give at least one *"little gift of joy"* to someone else every day. You will get so much joy yourself from finding ways to give gifts of joy to others that your life will take on new excitement and expectation. Be creative. You may see something that makes you smile, and you know someone else who would enjoy this, too. Give it to them.

For instance, there is a small bakery in Jackson, Tennessee that makes the most delicious cookies in beautiful shapes of butterflies, high-heeled shoes, flowers, etc. These have pretty, colored icing, all different colors that are so happy. Sometimes when I am in the area, I will go by and buy one just to give as a gift to a friend because they are such fun. For a small amount of money, this will bring great joy to someone. The gift is that you were thinking of that person, not how much the gift costs.

You might see a book that you feel someone would love and send it to them. I have a neighbor who will bring me a bouquet of roses from her rose garden. This makes me happy, for I can't seem to grow roses. My garden is too shady for one reason, and another reason is roses take lots of time and care. The thing here is to pay attention to others—what they like, what they enjoy—and be thoughtful of them. This means you have noticed them and know what they like, and that is a great compliment. Any time we get outside of ourselves and do for others, this is good for the world around us as well as for ourselves.

You have probably been around someone who all they ever talk about is themselves or their immediate family. After a while, this grows old, doesn't it? Remember this when you are talking. Keep the topic off of yourself so much. Ask people questions about themselves and be interested. Get outside of yourself and talk to them about their lives, their interests. Be aware of going on and on about yourself, your problems, your issues, what you think, and your interests only. Think of others. Care about others and their wants, their likes, their needs. Look them in the eye when you listen or speak to them. Show them you care. Most people are fighting hard in this world and doing the best they can at this moment. Try not to judge or to be critical; just be there for them. They may not be doing it as you would, but that is okay. Love them anyway. Accept them where they are in God's love. They may have had the life knocked out of them. Help put life back into them. This will also keep abundant life in you.

When you've had the life knocked out of you, pull yourself up again and get some fun out of life! Fight back!

⊶⊷

CHAPTER 29

Sprinkle Joy Throughout Your Day

*P*lan fun things into every day, as I have said before. Have things for which you look forward. Every morning, write a "joy" into your day and then do it. This will keep you looking forward to what's ahead. You may read some in a good book for thirty minutes sometime that day, or stop at a special spot—be it in your flower garden, a park, or a favorite café—and have a cup of coffee. Or it might be to walk through a shop where you love to browse. You may visit someone you enjoy seeing, or have lunch at a favorite restaurant. Give yourself a treat of joy during your day. You might want to purchase a flower for your desk or beside your bed. Anything that will bring you a smile and a moment of joy and pleasure will do. Sprinkle joy throughout your day just like sunshine. This simple exercise will brighten and cheer you every day. It is easy to do, if you will just do it. This will change your entire attitude and your day, every day. Do not allow yourself to get too busy to do this. Make this a "joy habit" for yourself.

"Each morning we are born again. What we do today is what matters most."

- Buddha

This day, this new day, you can begin again—afresh, anew. Each of us has the power within ourselves, with God's help, to make this day a day of joy, of love, of giving, of doing good. We can make the world a better place for ourselves and for others. Never think you are insignificant because you are not! You matter to God; you matter to others who come in contact with you this day; you matter in the world.

"Ye are here to be salt of the earth . . . . Ye are the light of the world."

- Matthew 5:13-14

"Everything that lives, lives not alone, nor for itself."

- William Blake

You do make a difference in the corner of the world where you live every day. Make certain it is a difference for good.

"As Christians, we can't love the whole world. But we should remember that God has placed us in a specific community at a particular time. We're called to love those around us. Loving them means serving them—and in doing so, we become the best of citizens."

- C. S. Lewis

Brighten up your life and the life of those around you. Live as lovingly and as joyfully as you can where you are right now.

For those who know me, they are aware I celebrate my birthday for a whole month. I call it my "birthday month," and I'm considering expanding and starting having a "birthday year." I hear some people say, "Oh, I don't celebrate birthdays. I don't want to think about them." Well, I personally believe this is crazy thinking! You are going to have birthdays as long as you are living, so you might as well enjoy them! I expect presents throughout the month (one a day, at least), and I give myself presents if no one else does. It's a fun time—my birthday month. You might want to celebrate this way yourself. It's joy! The other alternative to having birthdays is to die, so I choose to celebrate life!

I received an invitation to a surprise birthday party for a friend of mine. Her husband had sent the invitations and had written on the bottom of the invitation, "No presents, please." Well, I told David never to put that on an invitation to one of my parties. I wanted presents, and the more the merrier!!! I love to give gifts, and I love to receive gifts. It doesn't have to cost lots of money. The gift may be a one dollar item wrapped in a pretty package. The fun is the giving and receiving of the gift itself. Celebrate and live life happily!

My sister, who now has a "birthday month" herself, is one of the most thoughtful and giving people I know. Anytime she comes to visit, she always brings a bag full of little gifts or "little happys" we call them. When she was a girl, she loved to unwrap presents. One of the games she always wanted to play was for me to wrap things from the house and she would unwrap them. She still loves to unwrap things, so she comes bearing gifts all wrapped up because she also enjoys seeing others enjoy this. And her gifts are always the most thoughtful, greatest things. She pays attention to people, listens, and knows what they like and enjoy.

Again, it doesn't have to be terribly expensive to be the greatest gift, but when a gift is given out of love and you know someone really thought of you when they gave the gift, that is part of the gift. Gift giving is an art and can bring joy to both the giver and the receiver. Don't you just love the feeling you get when you find the perfect gift for someone, and how you look forward to seeing them open their gift? Keep a lookout for little gifts you can get for someone to brighten their day. Give a "*little gift of joy*" to yourself and to someone else today!

CHAPTER 30

Get In On The Party

$\mathcal{M}$ any of the memories I have made with my children and grandchildren center around the holidays. We always try to have an Easter egg hunt, and even though the grandchildren are now growing older, they still seem to think this is fun. In the autumn, we have a hot dog roast, hayride, and bonfire out in the country. We may have to change some of the festivities and make them more teenage or young adult friendly, but they still want to get together as a family and do these things. Adjust as you need to and yet remain the same. By this I mean keep things fun for all ages as the children grow up, but still celebrate together and share in times of fun and festivities.

You may have to rearrange your time of doing things to accommodate a growing family. When your children marry, they become part of another family as well as yours. You will have to share them. Maybe you have always had Christmas morning with your children, but now their new in-laws want to have them come to their house Christmas morning. You can choose to pout, get your feelings hurt, and cause your child pain and trouble, or decide to be flexible and modify your tradition to flow into your child's new life. Life has to have lots of give-and-take. It is not easy, and I won't say it is. If you rearrange your schedule, your traditions to help the growing family, you will come out the winner because you will have family around who want to be there, who love being with you, and who appreciate that you were willing to sacrifice and give for them because you love them.

As the family grows and babies come along, there will be even more need to alter and adapt. Your children may choose to spend their holidays in their home with their own children. They may invite you, and they may not. Remember, "Bend, don't break." Breathe, relax, and think before you speak.

There is also sometimes the problem of divorced parents and the issue of who gets to be with the children at what time. You need to try, as the parent, to make it as easy on the children as you can, knowing they didn't cause the situation. It was not their fault, and yet they often struggle because of this. Think of others. Be kind and as flexible as you can during these times. Holidays are often the most stressful times of the year because of family issues. You may be sad and alone on some holidays, but don't put a guilt trip on your children. Plan something fun for yourself and get over yourself. Try to be happy for them as well as for yourself.

We, as the parents, may need to rethink our traditions and the way "we have always done it" and celebrate completely differently this year. I now say "we don't have to celebrate on the actual holiday. We can make our holiday anytime we want it to be. The main thing is to be together and enjoy."

You may have your Thanksgiving Day celebration a month before or after the actual holiday. You may take a family cruise for Christmas rather than your usual get-together. Everyone can't be at every celebration? Well then, change the celebration to another time, or go ahead with the ones who can come and have fun. Be flexible as your life changes. If you don't, you will be left behind, alone and disappointed.

You can either get in on the party of life or not come to the party. It's your choice. As for me, I want to be at the party!

No one wants to be around a self-centered person who is so set in their own ways and won't do anything but what they have always done. Maybe you will say or think, "Well, that is the way I like it, and that is the way I want to live my life." Then by all means, do it your way and live your life. That is your choice and perfectly okay, but you will also have to accept the fact that you may do it your way—alone. Your family and friends may choose not to be with you as you live your life the way you want. If you want them around, you will have to change a little and sometimes do it their way. Life just works better with give-and-take.

I know I want to get in on the party!

CHAPTER 31

Set Your Mood For The Day

*Y*ou can choose to drift through your days and just get through, or you can decide to celebrate the day. It is all up to you—your attitude, your responsibility. When you wake, you have an option to either be happy or to be sad. Why would anyone make a conscious decision to be sad? I don't know, but some days we do. If we have this choice, and we do, let us choose wisely and happily.

One of the reasons, I believe, that we sometimes make an unwise pick is because of what we have allowed to come into our minds. We listen to bad news on the television or read about it first thing in the morning in our newspaper, or we listen to harsh, bad music. Think—really think—about what you allow to enter your mind as you start your day. It sets your mood for the entire day.

Make an effort to start your day with something uplifting and encouraging. Read something good: an inspirational quote, a writer you enjoy, or listen to music that is calming, happy, or upbeat. Also, watch what you say and do in the mornings. Make your words a positive affirmation to those around you. This is especially true for those who have children still at home. Make their mornings happy ones.

Encourage and uplift yourself and those around you. You may not be a "morning person," but try, really try, to start your day in a positive manner. It will make a difference for your entire day. It will make a difference to those who are around you. Spread joy all around you. Give "*little gifts of joy*" all day long. You can change your world every day by doing this. You can make a big difference in your world. This simple practice can make your world so much happier. Try it— you'll like it!

Make it your habit to look for the good as you go throughout your day. I know you have known people who see the worst in everything, in everybody. Be the opposite of this. See the good in everybody, in everything that happens. When bad happens, look for what you can learn from this. Find the good. This may be difficult, and sometimes it will take time to see the good. It may take years before we realize, "Yes, there was some good that came from that bad time in my life."

> "Look for the good instead of the bad, the right instead of the wrong, the beauty instead of the blight, the joy instead of the sorrow. Do this, and you'll always have something good to say."

> - Hal Urban

"Every day that we wake up is a good day. Every breath that we take is filled with hope for a better day. Every word that we speak is a chance to change what is bad into something good."

- Walter Mosley

Yes, every day that we are given is a blessing, a gift, so we should celebrate and look at it in that light. "Hip-Hip-Parade!" Let the celebrations begin!

If you will think of this day as your precious gift, you will cherish and appreciate it and find joy in the day. Find the joy today; it is there if you will look. What a wonderful and uplifting revelation. It is so simple, but true. We are given so many blessings, and we often waste them simply by not noticing them as blessings. Wake up and "count your blessings!"

It may be that you have obligations—things to do you really don't want to do this day. We all have these feelings at times. But it is up to us to make the best of what we have to do. Go at it with a different outlook. Do it; don't dread it and put it off. Go for it with as much joy as you can. Make your work as good as you can. Readjust your attitude toward your work and those with whom you work, if your attitude is bad. Do things in a atypical way. Transform your thinking and make over your life at work, or anywhere for that matter. Make your work space your own, a place that brings you joy, whether it be the type of file folders you use, the pens with which you write, putting fresh flowers on your desk—do things that make the area unique just for you.

Make a point to watch your speech to those in your workplace, pay special attention to others, ask about them, and do something nice for them— even those who make you mad. Yes, your attitude toward them can become new when you think in a more positive way toward them and try to look for something good in them. Often when we just don't like someone, we let this attitude grow, fester, and become worse and worse, rather than trying to modify our own attitude. It will make our lives better if we can look for the good and major on that. Instead of majoring and often obsessing on others' mistakes, instead try to find some right things they do and bring it to light.

> "Never react emotionally to what happens but always look for and find in every situation the good that's surely present there."

> - Norman Vincent Peale

Just as we have a choice to create the life we live by our words and actions or reactions, we have a choice by the way we treat those around us to improve their day, their life, and our workplace or home. We can make our life and the lives of those around us more joyful. Just think of the power within you to do this. It is amazing and wonderful!

> Watch your thoughts; they become words.
> Watch your words; they become actions.
> Watch your actions; they become habit.

Watch your habits; they become character.
Watch your character; it becomes your destiny.

- Frank Outlaw

When you think thoughts of joyfulness, think on good and have this inner peace; your life is easier, less stressful, and much more fun. This is the easiest type of existence—a more relaxed, joy-filled life. You have within you the power to live this serene, blissful life.

"The way to happiness: keep your heart free
from hate, your mind from worry. Live simply, expect little, and give much. Fill your life
with love. Scatter sunshine. Forget self, think
of others. Do as you would be done by. Try
this for a week and you will be surprised."

- H. C. Mattern

"Where God and love are there is happiness.
So a practical principle in creating happiness is
to practice love."

- Norman Vincent Peale

CHAPTER 32

Never A Dull Moment

*N*ever allow your life to become dull. Keep your life bubbling with joy. Maintain your energy by what you focus on, what you read, what you hear, what you do, where you go, and the people you are around.

Stretch yourself. Celebrate your life daily! Do not allow doubts and fears to enter your daily life. Go for life all out—full throttle! If you believe in yourself and keep your motives pure, you will overcome and succeed each day of your life.

Pray. Ask God for guidance, strength, wisdom, and help in all you do, then plunge ahead. We lose our energy when we allow our thinking, our life to become dull and colorless. Paint exciting pictures in your mind of things you want to accomplish.

Think calm, act calm! Always remind yourself to go calmly and joyfully along in life. Appreciate the good in your life. It's your own fault if your enthusiasm is waning. You yourself must feed and nurture your own enthusiasm. Rejoice and celebrate everything! Make a party out of it. Play often and find ways to enjoy your own company.

There won't always be other people around. Even when we are alone, we can be enthusiastic! Look for things you love to do. Think about this. It may be that you love sitting and looking at a magazine, writing a letter, reading, listening to music, looking at beautiful scenery—something you enjoy alone. Do this and enjoy. You may love activities such as walking, running, skating, biking, or boating. Stretch yourself beyond your comfort zone. There are going to be times in our lives when we will be alone and quiet, whether we want to or not, so we need to learn how to handle these times and discover how to enjoy our own company.

Personally, I have found books to be good friends to me during alone time. Now that alone times are good to me, I find I want more and more time alone. I sometimes now have to push myself to be around people. There is a happy and healthy medium here. We all need people: friends, family, co-workers, and other human contact.

Some people always have noise around them. They don't like complete quiet. I personally enjoy quiet, but I know some who have to have the television or music playing at all times. You may want to work on this a little at a time; just give yourself a few minutes of quiet several times a day. Quietness helps us stay calm, helps us focus, helps connect us to nature, helps us to pray, meditate, and to practice our deep breathing. Often we are rushing so through our day that we don't notice our breathing or anything else we are doing. To be quiet and calm in our day is good and healthy for us. Make a practice of this every day of your life. Take time. Make time for quiet.

Even just a few minutes will help you clear your mind of troubles. Relax, breathe deeply, and pay attention to your breathing—in and out, in and out. Think on good thoughts, happy thoughts, uplifting and encouraging thoughts. "What you think—you become," writes Norman Vincent Peale, and I truly believe this. What we habitually think on and dwell on is what we become. Make it your habit to think good thoughts. When you catch yourself slipping and thinking negatively, thinking failure, or thinking sad thoughts or thoughts of worry, change your thoughts. Stop the process and rethink using "joy." Rather than thinking failure, think success. Rather than down thoughts, think up thoughts. Rather than thinking no, think yes. After a while, you will see this does work. Oh, it is not an overnight change, and you may have to work on this throughout your entire life, but it's worth the effort. We have a choice to think what we want and to become who we want. It is up to us.

I am not leaving God out when I say this, but I believe God gives us a choice and wants us to choose the joyful way. He is not going to make us be joyful, but we can choose joy. It is there for every one of us.

> "The wonderful thing about it is we have a choice. We can smolder on the dark side, or flourish on the bright side."

> - Norman Vincent Peale

I choose to flourish, don't you? It is all in the way we decide to live our life. Go joyfully through your days looking for the good, for the "*little gifts of joy*" each precious day holds for you. Even on your worst days, there are moments where you can find joy if you will watch and pay attention. What you expect out of life you will usually find. Make it your goal to never have a dull moment—quiet moments yes, but never dull!

CHAPTER 33

Dream: Ready-Set-Go!

One of my dreams, after my husband and I bought our Main Street Cottage, was to have a bridge built across the creek that runs behind our house, in order to access our land on the other side of the creek.

One year, for my Christmas present, David and our grandson, Austin, built my dream bridge. It is great fun to stand on the bridge, walk across to the other side, or to sit and think, relax, or have a picnic. They made it wide enough so that I could put a small table and two chairs on it and have a picnic there, right on the bridge.

It is my quiet place—a place of joy to me—and a dream come true. Remember when I said earlier in this book, "If you don't dream and make plans, nothing will happen?" I write about this to share with you a real dream that I had come true because I dared to dream the dream. This was no small dream or small bridge. The span across the creek is forty-five feet, so this was quite a task David and Austin undertook. It was a big dream and a big gift they gave to me, and I was so grateful and filled with love and thankfulness to them for doing this for me.

This was one of the most wonderful and special gifts I have ever received. If I had never dared to dream and ask for this, it would never have happened. Dream your dreams and plan for them to come true. They just might! You never know until you try. For those of you who knew my David, you know he tried to make everyone's dreams come true. He was the most loving and giving person I have ever known. He did for everyone, not just for me.

One day, my mother and I were talking about David and all he did for friends, neighbors, and family and she said, "What would this neighborhood do without David?" Then she added, "What would our family do without David?" Sadly, we have had to learn to live without David, but his spirit, love, and generosity are sorely missed. People could count on him to help, and he was always there for others. I was blessed to have him in my life, and that's another dream come true! If you don't ask, you won't receive.

Believe in your dreams and dream big; pray, ask, believe, and plan. Then work hard to make those dreams come true. Often we have to work to make our dreams a reality. They will not always just be given to us as a gift. Work for what you want. Work is good for us. It will make us feel a sense of accomplishment and self-worth and give us pride in ourselves. When things come too easily to us, we often don't appreciate them as we should. Appreciation and gratefulness are good traits to have. Always be grateful and appreciative for everything that comes your way.

Only you can make your dreams come true. Don't wait for someone else to make things happen. You have this dream, so work toward it. Work, pray, and go for it. You are here on earth for only a short time in the real scheme of things, so make plans, have your dreams, and work toward making those dreams a reality. Determine within yourself to live a happy life. You can if you desire to do so. Think on your strengths. Be kind and encouraging to yourself and to others. Be around other people who are cheering and uplifting.

> "A single conversation across the table with a wise man is better than ten years study of books."

> - Henry Wadsworth Longfellow

Be in the company often of people who are wise, uplifting, heartening, and loving. These people will help lift you, keep you motivated, and aid you in reaching your goals and dreams. Surround yourself with people who lift you up, who inspire you, who stretch you, and assist you to become a better person. In the same way, you yourself strive to be of assistance, uplift, and motivate those around you. Always care about others and their needs, wants, and dreams, and give of yourself, your time, and your talents.

Strive to be trustworthy and be around people who are trustworthy. Who your friends are says a lot about you. You become like those with whom you associate. Pay close attention to what people are saying and doing. If it feels wrong for you, stay away.

Become aware of what you say and do. Your character, your actions, and who you are inside will shine through if you pay attention. You can change yourself if you don't like who you are becoming. Always strive to become who you want to be. The life you dream for yourself can be yours. You can be as happy and as joyful as you want to be. Live well. Share your joy of life with those around you.

> "Sorrow shared is halved and joy shared is doubled."

> - Native American Saying

You can go about sharing your joy-filled spirit every day, wherever you go. Make a point, a habit of being a "joy-spreader." As you go, spread joy! Nothing is stopping you. Begin. Right now—today—this very moment.

Determine what's important to you. Once you know this, then you can accomplish much. As you work toward what's critical to you, you will work happily and creatively. Set a goal, a dream, and forward toward that.

> "Rejoice today for all you have been given and live in a state of rejoicing. Joy is a result, not a goal."

> - Alexandra Stoddard

Live your potential and constantly be looking to see your great potential. We all have much more ability than we are using. When one is quiet and searches, one can find those abilities, those talents, those things in life you want to do but have never tried before. You are never too young or too old to become what you should become. Forget about age. I have heard of unbelievable things being accomplished by very young children in this world, and I've also heard of those who found their life's true talent and became fulfilled and famous after sixty or seventy years of age. We should forget age and just do it!

> "What we become depends not on conditions but on decisions."
>
> - Hal Urban

The decisions we make determine our outcome. We make up our mind to be joyous, to live our dreams, to plan, and then do or not do. Make a plan, and then start working toward that goal. This gets our lives going. So decide and then start! Do not talk yourself out of your dreams. Pray always and ask God for wisdom and help, but then if you feel this is the right thing, go for it. And go for it in a big way. Be courageous. Be fearless. Be enthusiastic. Be passionate. Do not be afraid to fail. At least you tried. Success is getting up when we have failed, shaking it off, and trying again. Keep on keeping on. Do not allow yourself, your spirit, to be defeated.

"The only limitations we have are the ones put on us, first by others and then by ourselves. They exist because we believe them."

- Hal Urban

This, I believe, is so true. We buy into the notion that we can't do something because we have either been told this by someone else, or we have convinced ourselves that we can't. Listen to this. We have convinced ourselves by telling ourselves over and over we aren't worthy, we can't, we don't deserve it, and on and on it goes. Good things can and often do happen to us if we are looking for the good, the "*little gifts of joy*" out there in this world. So look for the good, look for the joy, look for the best to happen to you.

This is the way to live victoriously and joyfully here and now—right now —not tomorrow, but now. As you go along looking for the good, the joy, the excellent things to happen, you will find good things are happening in your life now, and you can build on these daily. One good thing will lead to another. You will share your joy and happiness with those around you and it will spread. Always be on the lookout for the good, and it is amazing what will happen. You will find what you are seeking. You will find the good.

Make joyful plans and dream. If you don't make plans, nothing will happen in your life. You will go through life day by day anyway, so you might as well make plans to accomplish something as you go. What do you want to achieve? It may be a wild dream you think, but never allow anyone to discourage your dream. Make plans and then go for it! It is better to try and keep trying than to never go for your dreams. Remember, the difference between a success and a failure is that the successful tried just one more time.

You may have to try a different way the next time, take a different route, rethink your plan, reevaluate and restructure, but go for your dream. Your dreams may change over the years as you grow and mature. You may not want the same thing now that you once did. So what? You are in charge of your dreams. Redefine them if you wish. This does not mean you have failed. This just means you have made a bend, turned a corner on your road of life, and your view has now altered. You may have many dreams and plans as you go through life. Some of them you will reach and some you may not, but the plan is to enjoy your life, to do some good, and grow as a person as you go along. Always grow and go forward. Don't ever throw away your time regretting. Regret is a big waste of your precious, wonderful time here on earth.

You are the one in charge of your choices, so choose wisely to be happy and do good. A particular situation may not go the way you would have liked, but look at it and make the best out of it. It may not be perfect, but you will possibly learn something from the situation, or it will help someone else. Everything is not always about you or me all the time. We must think of others, too. When I say "be happy and be joyful," this does not mean to be selfish, self-centered, and consider no one other than yourself. To be a truly joyful individual, one must be loving, giving, kind, and think of others. I just mean live while you live, and live as happily and joyfully as you possibly can every moment. Look at all the good that is happening around you. Look for the "*little gifts of joy*" throughout your day, and soon you will be noticing those more than any bad things. Major on the joys!

During rough times, know that joy will come again, so hang in there! Train your mind to think on the good, even when difficulty comes. Very little is needed to have a happy life if one is content with oneself. Look for the things in life that bring you lasting joy. Pay attention to what is happening inside you, what you are thinking, what you are feeling. Do you feel rushed and scattered? Your body may be telling you to slow down, to relax, to do stress-relieving exercises, to take a walk, or to sit in a calm, quiet place and recharge your soul. Do you feel pulled in a million different directions? Stop and think. You can, in actuality, only do one thing at a time well. This multi-tasking thing is just not true. It is only mind swapping back and forth from one thing to another, which often leads to scattered energy and tired minds. Decide what is important. What is the more needful task to you at this time? Prioritize, possibly delegate, and maybe you can actually let some things go completely. You don't have to do everything yourself, do you? If you were no longer here, it wouldn't get done by you, would it? If you keep pushing yourself and stressing yourself, you may not be here in reality. Think about this. Is "it" really worth a heart attack, a stroke, or a nervous breakdown? I didn't think so. No one—not even you—can be all things to all people and do it all. Go easy on yourself. Please!

We often hear and tell ourselves to do the best we can, and I tell myself this often. But doing the best you can never means killing yourself. Be your most excellent and then let it go!

CHAPTER 34

Manners — The Happy Way Of Doing Things

*A*lways remember to thank others for what they do for you. Remember in first grade, kindergarten, or even earlier, when we were taught to say "please and thank you?" These are still good rules today.

"Manners are the happy way of doing things."

- Unknown

People everywhere like to be appreciated, thanked, recognized, loved, and accepted. We all do. So be conscious of this and say thank you, write a note of encouragement, tell others you appreciate something they did. Bless others and bless yourself.

People who are thankful show their attitude of joy for the gifts they receive. Be a cheerful giver and a cheerful receiver. We love to give a gift and have the one who receives the gift really show they love it, don't we? Yes, of course we do. It makes us happy when we see they appreciate and love what we chose to give them. That is a gift back to the giver in itself. Remember this the next time you receive a gift. Accept it graciously, lovingly, and joyfully, letting the giver know you truly appreciate their thoughtfulness in giving you this very special gift.

Parents, please teach your children to be thankful and to say please and thank you. They are kind and great words to use every day. They are powerful words. Let us never forget our manners. These three words—please, thank you—with a smile added, can do more to open doors for people than any other words. They can turn strangers into friends, turn cold into warmth, change attitudes, and brighten up a dark day. Try it; you might be pleasantly surprised.

Open up your heart. Be grateful. Be thankful. Smile. Look someone in the eye and say a meaningful please or thank you. It works. It truly does. Live your life graciously and mannerly.

Always be sensitive and respectful of the needs of others. We parents should teach our children to be thoughtful of others by our words as well as our actions. Respect for another human being is of the utmost importance. Without it, we are out of control, thoughtless, and out for disaster.

> "Our rewards in life will always be in exact proportion to the amount of consideration we show toward others."

> - Earl Nightingale

"Without good manners human society becomes intolerable and impossible."

- George Bernard Shaw

I know you have probably been in a public place and have witnessed someone being rude and causing a scene. Every time this happens, it makes the person causing the scene look foolish and rude, and it embarrasses those with and around them. We should always behave in such a way that if later a video or picture of us were shown, we would not be ashamed of it. In today's society, where most everyone has a camera on their phone, this could easily happen. We need to be in control of ourselves. There are times when we might be in the right and someone else is out of control with us, but we always have the power over how we respond. Remember, an argument can't happen unless there are two participating. You are in command if you rule over your own emotions. Don't give your emotions over to anyone else. Speak calmly if you can, or you can always walk away. You may think this is the coward's way, but really, it is often much more difficult.

". . . all things whatsoever ye would that men should do to you, do ye even so to them. . . ."

- Matthew 7:12

Life is much too short to allow ourselves to be upset by "stupid" things that really matter very little in the big scheme of things. Ten years from now, will it really matter? In eternity, will it matter? Now these two questions answered yes may be worth standing up for, but not worth losing your temper and behaving badly. The one who prays and remains calm usually wins in the long run. Maybe we won't win the immediate or short battle, but in the long-term, yes. Remember: you are in charge of your own behavior at all times and in every situation.

> "Life is as fleeting as a rainbow, a flash of lightning, a star at dawn. Knowing this how can we quarrel?"
>
> - Buddha

Yet, we do quarrel, don't we? Or we have confrontations with those who disagree with us or upset us. There are mean-spirited and hurtful people in this world, and often we have to be in their presence. But we can choose our response to them. We can stay in a loving place if we will notice our thoughts and keep in control of our own attitudes and responses. There can be no quarrel if we aren't quarreling, can there? Step back, be quiet, breathe, relax, calm yourself, and refocus on how you wish to respond. The disposition of people around us has an effect on us. There are some people we should stay away from if possible. Some we may have to be around, but we must reevaluate our reaction and responses to them. Check your attitude. This can make you stronger, a better person. We should try to be extra kind to people who are ill-tempered, frazzled, and on edge. They have some issues they are dealing with, and maybe our kindness, our smile, or our calmness will help them today.

The way we act or react shows our core being, what's really inside us. When you are shaken, what spills out? No one can disturb your center, your core, unless you allow it.

If you sometimes fail, you can ask forgiveness and try again. I have failed at this many times throughout my life. I have been told I have a temper—and my temper has often won—but I am trying and working on this. As I grow older, I feel I am finally learning this life lesson more fully. I pray so, anyway. Keep on trying until you master this. I will, too.

CHAPTER 35

Stay Outside The Storm

"The storms of life don't have to get inside us."

- Alexandra Stoddard

*I*t has often been advised to people under extreme stress to have their minds take them somewhere peaceful. This is supposed to help calm them. It has worked for me. When I have been in a dentist's chair and starting to become anxious, I have closed my eyes, breathed deep and slow, and thought of myself sitting in the swing on my grandmother's back porch with her beside me. I always felt safe and loved there with her. It is my peaceful, safe place to go in my mind, and it has calmed my anxieties many times. This has helped keep the storms of life outside of me.

Once, when I had an accident and was placed by paramedics on a back board and strapped down, I felt myself start to panic. I closed my eyes, breathed slow and deep, and started to pray for peace and calm. I went to that safe place in my mind— to my grandmother's porch. It didn't take all the anxiety away, but it did cause me to relax enough to get through this. Until that time, I had not realized I had a problem with tight spaces.

Often when we are in a storm of life, we just need to step away from it for a time. Possibly, we need to go to a quiet place alone for a few minutes to pull our thoughts together. You know an argument cannot occur unless there are two people. Simply refuse to join in an argument. Try to remain loving and gracious in your attitude. Remain peaceful inside. Do not allow the storm to get inside you. Keep your inner self calm no matter what is happening around you on the outside.

When you are confronted with a major problem—maybe a health crisis, or a family crisis—breathe, pause, shut your eyes, and go to that quiet, safe place before you react or speak. In times of crisis, you may say something in a moment of panic or hurt that you cannot undo or unsay, something that might hurt someone else needlessly. Pause and do not let anything unloving spill out of you. Try to keep yourself outside of the storm. Stay in the calm zone.

CHAPTER 36

Define Your Life

"The kind of life we want depends on the kind of people we are—on our character."

- Robert Bellah

What kind of life do you want? This is a deep and thought-provoking question, but one we need to ask ourselves often because ultimately, we get the life we want. Now I know that bad things often happen to good people, but often we get what we plan toward, what we really want. You may read this statement and totally disagree, but please, I ask you to sit quietly and think on this awhile. We are either our own worst enemy or our own best advocate. We choose a lot of our life by our own actions, thoughts, etc. We may have had a good or bad childhood. That part we can't choose or control, except for our thoughts. When we become adults, we do have choices.

I have seen people who had awful childhoods overcome them by their thinking and actions and bring themselves out.

I have seen others—who had seemingly wonderful child-hoods—become lazy, arrogant, resentful, and have unfulfilling lives. What is the difference?

I don't know. It's possibly their attitudes, their inside character. I do not claim to understand this. I really believe that we choose how we react. We can change the circumstances of our lives if we want by our attitude and our reaction. Modify your thinking. Adjust your reaction. Amend your attitude and completely change your life.

How we respond to others greatly affects how they respond to us. You don't like how someone is treating you? Respond to them differently. Only you can do this, and it may be very difficult. Years of reacting or responding in a certain way may have formed a deeply embedded habit in you. You may have to really think this through and plan ahead for the response you choose to make. Be prepared. It may take several tries for this to have a different outcome. You can change your attitude and response, and in doing so, you will most likely effect the entire dynamics of your relationship with this person.

This may be frightening to do. It can be hard and often scary because we aren't certain of the outcome. If you want something different than what you now have, you have a chance to make it so.

People, and our relationships with them, are a very important part of our lives. People define success differently. I sat down in a quiet place with pen and paper and wrote what I felt success in life to be, what was most important to me. This took me a long time, and I went back to it different days and at different times and changed the wording or added new thoughts. It is a work in progress still; however, I do think this is a good exercise for everyone to do. What's most important to you? How do you define success?

If we define success as living life fully, savoring each moment, this is good for our health. When we work such long hours at stressful jobs to make money for our concept of success, it can be a detriment to our health. Sometimes we allow television, magazines, movies, and the media to define what success is for us. In my opinion, feeling happy and fulfilled is success. I believe success to be loving and caring about yourself and others, having integrity, being truly yourself, and not pretending and living up to someone else's ideal of success.

We can get so busy making money, making a living, raising our family, just doing what has to be done to survive, that we don't stop and think of what is most important to us. What do we want our lives to be?

Think—really think—about the true meaning of life. Think about what is important to you, to your family, to your world. Everyday life often gets in our way. Taking a time-out to sit and think is a valuable and necessary part of a life. If you never do this, you will come to the end of your life simply having been pushed along with the flow and never having thought for yourself, never really having a thought fully on your own, only blindly agreeing with what you have been told by your culture, your upbringing, and your environment.

You may truly believe what you have been raised and taught to believe, but if you have taken the time to examine and find out why you do accept this, it will make you a stronger person with more firm beliefs. I know in my own life it was sometimes difficult to question or examine things closely, but afterwards, I felt a sense of deep peace and knew myself to be a stronger, more confident person.

Most all of us change as we grow older. But change is not always a bad thing. As we grow older, we should change into a more knowledgeable, more loving person. When we refuse to change and grow, we can become hardheaded, intolerant of others, selfish, and set in our ways.

I have learned much through my life and am certain there is more to learn; I am excited about what's ahead. As we grow older, we always say, "I wish I would have known this when I was younger." Oh well, I didn't, so I must just be glad I finally learned it and go forward with great hope of leaning more. One never grows too old to learn new things. That is a wonderful "*gift of joy*" God has given us—the ability to continue to learn.

Just think how very sad and hopeless life would be if when we reached a certain age there was nothing left to learn. There is plenty left to learn, so never stop learning and growing. This is a great joy in life. There are so many new places to go, to see, to learn about; so many new activities to do that you have never done before; so many people to help, to love, and encourage; so much more to learn in the world. Life is an exciting new adventure every day—a "*little gift of joy*" to open!

I heard this week about an older man, in his late eighties, who was giving away all his household "stuff," except for a very few items, moving across the country to be near his son, and entering an assisted living apartment. His wife had died several months ago. But rather than being sad and looking at this as the end of his life and being depressed, he was looking forward to this "great new adventure." He had loved his life and gave thanks for all he had done and had, but now he said he was excited to make new friends, have less "stuff" to take care of, have fewer responsibilities, and just enjoy a new chapter in his life. He had a great attitude, and everyone loved to be around him. I have no doubt that he will be happy in his new home and make new friends because people like to be around people like this. He had made the choice to be happy.

At the end of each day, if one can look back and say, "I have done some good today. I have been kind, loving, and truly cared about others as I have gone about my work and play. I made a good difference in the lives of someone," then you have succeeded that day.

> "One can only live happily ever after on a day-to-day basis."

> - Unknown

> "Happiness is like a butterfly which appears and delights us for a brief moment, but soon flits away."

> - Anna Pavlova

This is true. Moments of intense, beautiful happiness will come and go, but true joy in life can stay if it is inside us. Even when sorrows come into our lives, joy will spring up from within to help us through. Joy can be in our spirit, our inner being, in our very soul.

What does life mean to you? What and who in life is important to you? What do you want to do, to change, to learn? Who do you love and care about? These are the things and people you need to spend your time with. And now—right now—is the time to start. Define the life you want and then start working on it. The difference between a success and a failure is the successful person tries one more time. She (he) keeps keeping on and on.

> "Life is a succession of moments. To live each
> one is to succeed."

- Corita Kent

CHAPTER 37

Perseverance Is A Winner

*L*ife can be hard, but it can also be so wonderful! We learn, as we live our life, that everyone fails sometimes. There is no one who hasn't. So get over your failure and go on, once again. Don't let your failures defeat you.

Have you noticed people in public life—an actor, a politician, someone whom everyone watches—who may fail, make a terrible mistake, do something awful, and the whole world seems to turn against them? They really fall from grace in the public eye. But if you notice, the ones who just keep on going, hold up their heads, and continue on usually will come back into favor. Now, this may not happen if they continue to make the same mistakes over and over, but if they go on with their lives, smiling and trying, time heals and people seem to forgive. People know all of us fail sometimes, and we will forgive others for failures, too, if they keep on trying. Perseverance is a winner!

Learn from your failures and move on. Learning is the key. When we have learned, it really isn't a failure. It is when we refuse to learn anything that we have a big problem. Look at yourself, question why you did this, and possibly go another route. Change your destination, your choices, and pay careful attention. We always have a choice to do the right thing in every situation.

"Do all the good you can, by all the means you can."

- John Wesley

"Don't be afraid to fail. Don't waste energy trying to cover up failure. Learn from your failures, and go on to the next challenge. It's okay to fail. If you're not failing you're not growing."

- H. Stanley Judd

"The world breaks everyone and afterward many are strong at the broken places."

- Ernest Hemingway

"We can become stronger at our broken places if we choose to learn from our mistakes, correct our course, and try again."

- Hal Urban

"Success is how high you bounce after you hit bottom."

- General George S. Patton

We will fail sometimes in life. This is a certainty for everyone. But how we will respond to our failure is the real test. If we allow it to defeat us, then that is a real failure. If not, then a failure can turn into a victory, a learning and growing experience for us. If we are afraid to fail and don't ever step out and try this, it may be our biggest failure of all—never trying, never reaching for a goal, a dream. We need to learn that failing at something is not the worst that can happen. It is not the end of the world. We learn and we grow, and hopefully, we become a wiser and better person. Success very seldom comes the first time we try something, but only after much trial and error. We learn from our mistakes and then try again another day in another way. Never lose hope.

One of the reasons we may have setbacks is because we are going at such a frantic pace, trying to do everything and be everything to everybody. We get sidetracked or temporarily lose our purpose or take our eyes off our purpose. When we are trying to do too many things, we really don't do anything well. We need to concentrate, focus, pay attention to our task at hand, and put our energies into accomplishing that task. As a woman, you may have multiple responsibilities. You may be a mother, a wife, a professional, a caregiver; so many hats we wear in life. And this goes for men as well. You may have commitments to your family or your workplace or to others, and often this makes it very difficult to concentrate on just one thing. But you can really only do one thing at a time, so whatever your task is at the moment, concentrate and pay attention to that one thing at that time, and then move on to your next task. Do whatever you are doing at the time well. Switch tasks if you must, but pay close attention and focus on the one thing you are doing at that one moment, so as not to become scattered and do the job poorly.

> Isn't life glorious! Isn't it grand!
> Here—take it—hold it tight in your hand;
> Squeeze every drop of it into your soul,
> Drink of the joy of it, sun-sweet and whole!
> Laugh with the love of it, burst into song!
> Scatter its richness as you stride along!
> Isn't life splendid—and isn't it great
> We can always start living—it's never too
> late!

- Helen Lowrie Marshall

Figure out your priorities—what is really important to you— and then pay close attention to those people, those things you hold dear. I have said this over and over in this book. Weed out the nonessentials, the unimportant that clutter your life. Your life is glorious and grand! Drink in the joy now while you can. This may sound ridiculous to you. You may think there is just no way you can do this with your crazy, busy, mixed-up schedule and whirlwind of a world. The task seems daunting to one who is used to going in twenty different directions at one time. You can't imagine how to stop this and ever get anything accomplished. But if you will stop a minute, sit and calm yourself, prioritize your life, and let go of much that bogs you down, your life will gradually begin to become more tranquil, and you can find your joy, your peace, and get things done in a more efficient and joy-filled way.

CHAPTER 38

You Can't Be Everything To Everybody

"You don't have to do everything and be everything for everyone else all the time. If you think you can't possibly do one more thing without screaming or crying, you're probably right. Start by saying, "No, I'm sorry, I've got a prior commitment."

- Sarah Ban Breathnach

It is so true; you cannot be everything to everybody all the time. Realize this and give yourself a break. Be kind to yourself. Don't beat yourself up. Often we feel as if we are indispensable. That may make us feel needed and good for a while, but it often pushes us to abuse ourselves by doing too much, too fast all the time. We must realize when we are doing this to ourselves and stop this. Only we can stop it. No one else can do this for us.

Sometimes our bodies will tell us we are doing too much by shutting down, and we become ill. We must listen to our bodies and rest when needed, take slow down breaks, and rejuvenate our spirits and our bodies by being good to ourselves. Ultimately we can do more, be more when we are getting proper rest and treating our bodies and our minds correctly. We are more focused and productive in good ways when we take proper care of ourselves.

Today, while writing my book, was one of those days when my body was telling me to rest and be well. I caught a cold and felt under the weather. But rather than push myself, take some medicine, and go on, I decided to take the day off, stay in my pajamas all day and rest, read, write, and restore my soul. I was more tired than I had realized, having gone and gone recently, every day having to be somewhere for an appointment and rushing from point A to point B. When anyone called and asked me, I would just say "yes" and write them into my appointment book. This felt good, like I was accomplishing much, always needing to do something, be somewhere, rush, rush, rush! I got caught up in this and forgot my own advice, that is, until my body reminded me. So here I sit, sipping a cup of hot, spiced tea, enjoying the sunshine coming through the sunroom window on this cold, winter's day, resting and restoring. We all have to have days like this occasionally. Hopefully, I will do this again without having to have sickness remind me to do so. Even when we know better, we will often slip and not take proper care of ourselves. Take care of yourself as you are caring for everyone else in your life. Liking yourself and finding your own self-confidence is an essential element in life if you are to have joy.

We hopefully learn from our mistakes. We can learn lessons and great wisdom from living our life. Everything we have been through in life, everything we are now going through, is teaching us. We are growing and changing into an even more wonderful, loving person. Only you have lived through your life experiences, and while others may have similar experiences, yours are unique and the life lessons you have learned are yours. We can share our life stories with others to help and encourage them. When we reach out to another and share a little part of ourself, we reap benefits from this ourselves.

> "Always be a first-rate version of yourself, instead of a second-rate version of somebody else."

> - Judy Garland

Each of us was born into unique circumstances. We were born in a particular area of the world and were raised in a unique way. It may seem normal to us, but to others who were raised in a different culture with another belief system, it may seem strange. But you are you, and you have become who you are partly due to where you were born, how you were treated as a child, what you learned, what you were exposed to, and how you were loved or unloved.

When my father died, my mother, brother, sister, and I were sitting around Mother's dining table, looking at pictures and planning his funeral. It was a sad time, but also a good time as we looked at family photos, laughed, and remembered sweet times. We were talking about friends and family when Mother said something that made us all laugh out loud, and we have kept this as a "family saying." She said about someone's family, "Well, they're strange. They're not like us!" She was very serious, but the rest of us burst out laughing. I said, "Mother, do you think maybe we're the strange ones?" She quickly said "No." So now when we are talking about others who act unlike us, we say, "They're strange—they're not like us" and then burst into laughter. We all think we are "normal," don't we, whatever "normal" is.

We always tend to think we are the normal ones and the way other people live or think, if not similar to us, is strange. We may have special ways of thinking, dissimilar values and beliefs, distinctive ways of celebrating holidays, and varied ways of relating to others and reacting to circumstances. Now that our world has become so small with the Internet and television, and people from other countries moving all over the world for jobs, cultures all live in close proximity. People are seeing changes to which they were never before exposed.

When I was a child, most everyone in our town was of a similar social status, religion, had the same value systems, and so forth. It wasn't until I became an adult and moved to a larger city that I saw this change. We talk about dysfunctional families. I am not sure there were ever functional, or what one would call "normal" families, but just families with problems and issues who kept quiet about them. What is normal? I don't know. There comes a time in our lives when we choose who we want to become. To find one's "first-rate" version of "you" is usually an ongoing process, taking many years. Your "first-rate" you may change through the years. This is what is supposed to happen in life—change! Nothing stays the same. As we mature into adulthood, hopefully we will change and become our true, "first-rate" self. Our society is a difficult one in which to be one's self. We are constantly bombarded with TV and print ads showing so called "beautiful" people, and often we get caught up in looking, dressing, and acting as others. I am amazed when people say they are just expressing who they are and being "uniquely them," and then they are just dressing in the fads of the moment. We all tend to want to fit in; it just depends on what group we are fitting in with as to our dress and actions. To find your "first-rate" you, you may have to go through some of these fads, especially in your teen years.

Teen years are tough years, trying to find yourself, trying to be unique, and yet wanting to fit in at the same time. I won't even begin to suggest I understand these years. Hopefully you can face them with humor, from both sides, whether living through them yourself or knowing someone who is living through them. Just know that nothing is as serious and as awful as it seems at the time, and this, too, shall pass! Everything is of earth-shattering importance in these years. It is usually not. When you think about it, there are so many things we get all bent out of shape over that are truly just not worth our worry and anxiety in the total scheme of life. Having your way, winning an argument and such—does it really, really matter? Will your world be greatly affected by this one thing? Often friendships, relationships, and families are destroyed over small things that were not that major if you step back and look calmly at the entire situation from all sides. Are you emotional? Do you blow things out of proportion and end up making matters worse? If so, then you can change your reactions and actions if you wish to do this. It might make your life much less stressful, and you could live with less drama. Oh, I know some people enjoy drama in their lives. It makes them feel alive. It's all up to you and how you wish your life to be. But the main thing for you to do is to be your "first-rate" self, rather than trying to copy someone else. Remember, "You don't have to do everything and be everything for everyone else all the time."

CHAPTER 39

Don't Care—Never Will!

I have laughed over this statement made by a friend's four-year-old granddaughter. Her grandmother had given her a glass of milk to drink and then said to her, "Now Emma, don't spill your milk." Emma turned to her grandmother and said, "Don't care—never will!" Well, this may sound a bit disrespectful and sassy, but it struck me and her grandmother as funny. Because really, when you think about it, spilling a little milk is nothing earth-shattering. We adults make so many rules, and we should take a lesson from Emma and say "Don't care—never will" about many "unimportant" things in our life.

There are many situations that just aren't that important. Yet, we take them so seriously and wear ourselves out over them, when we should be saying "Don't care—never will." Think of this saying as you go through your life today. There are some things worth caring about, but many things just aren't that important and major.

We should take a lesson from a small child, lighten up, and not be too serious. Laugh and move forward. Spend your time caring about things that are of major importance, not so much those that are not. When things, problems, or some people scare you, look the thing, the problem, the person squarely in the eye and say, "Don't care—never will!" Often when we look at a problem—someone or something that is causing us undue stress, worry, or heartache—this reaction will set us free and is just what we need to say. "Don't care—never will, because frankly, it's not worth my care!"

Of course, this is way too simplistic for some things in life. Our relationships and the people we love and care about, cannot and should not be dismissed with "Don't care—never will." People we love and care for do often cause us pain and worry, and the issues may be such that we don't see how we are going to survive and live through the problems, which seem overwhelming. Faith and hope are all that get me through these kinds of hard times—and prayer, lots of prayer.

Today was one of those kinds of days, and as I was sitting at my desk— praying, writing, crying, and asking God to help— the church bells down the street from my house began playing an old song; a tune I recognized, and I sang along. The words gave great hope, and these lifted me. This I took as encouragement and strength. It was an answer to my prayers this morning. Sometimes we just need to stop and listen to things around us. I was thankful!

Worry actually can make a situation worse than it really is. It is about what might be and may never even happen. Your worst fears may never materialize, but thinking and obsessing on this may hurt your health, and it most certainly will steal your joy. Worry never (NEVER) changes anything! But I know how difficult—almost impossible—it is not to worry. When you start to worry, recognize it as worry and change your thinking, change your thoughts and actions into thoughts of joy, thoughts of blessings, thoughts of thankfulness, and prayer. Read something uplifting, sing a song out loud, or listen to calming, happy music. Change your response to worry.

I personally struggle with this problem big time. God has shown me over and over, time after time, that He will take care of me, and I will still forget this and start to worry and fret. Life will always—and I mean always—hold problems and things for you to worry over, but we must rise above these problems and cares. We can if we continue to try. And maybe the "Don't care—never will" attitude is good to use about the mundane, annoying things of life that sometimes get us down.

> "Any fact facing us is not as important as our attitude toward it, for that determines our success or failure."
>
> - Norman Vincent Peale

> "When the hurricane situations of life buffet us, the storm surges of emotion threaten to overwhelm, and the debris of our fragmented lives swirl around us, it is essential to connect

with a deeper, stronger force that is not over-whelmed by the chaos and change of outer events."

- Candy Paull

CHAPTER 40

Trust

"Look to God to be your source of good, not other people. Choose to trust God to bring good out of the most unpromising situations."

- Candy Paull

*T*rust. This is something that is often difficult to do. Possibly you have been hurt or disappointed by someone you once trusted, and you have lost your ability to really open up and trust.

Know that we all cause others pain sometimes. We may not mean to do this, but we may have hurt or disappointed someone ourselves. We must forgive others and forgive ourselves. We humans just aren't perfect. We mess up. Don't be too hard on others who have hurt you. They may have not meant to and feel bad about it themselves. We need to forgive, trust, and love.

"You cannot control what the other person says or does, but you can change your response, decide to have a different response, a different reaction, and make better choices."

- Candy Paull

"He who angers you conquers you."

- Proverb

"Life appears to me too short to be spent in nursing animosity or registering wrong."

- Charlotte Bronte

In the same way, he who hurts you, and you don't forgive and let it go, conquers you.

Like I have said before in this book, over and over, all people have problems, hurts, and burdens. Learning to deal with your problems is an ongoing job in life. No one's family or upbringing was perfect, but as long as there is love, acceptance, and encouragement in a home, there is great hope. If you were raised without love and acceptance, hopefully as you grow, you can love and accept yourself as you deserve to be loved and accepted.

Do not live with hate and unforgiveness, but instead choose love, trust, and hope. Then plan and live a better life. You can make your life and the lives of those around you better by your attitude, your strength of character, and your words and deeds. Always choose joy and give and receive "*little gifts of joy.*"

Why spend your precious time on this earth regretting something that has passed—possibly something you had no control over. Or why waste your time worrying, fretting, envying, or being jealous of what others may have, or holding a grudge and being unforgiving? Life is too precious and dear for these negative feelings and thoughts. Instead, when you feel yourself going in this direction, stop yourself and choose another way, another feeling, a different way of thinking.

Choose today to live your life and make it a good one. Oh, things will never be perfect; accept this fact. But live as best you can with as much love and joy as possible. Do the best in your power, with God's help, and then let go! It is a wonderful life if you will allow it to be. Live your life and open daily your "*little gifts of joy.*"

"Now the God of hope fill you with all joy. . ."

- Romans 15:13

Acknowledgments

I am thankful to many people who have encouraged and helped me throughout the book writing and publishing process. To my family for your belief in me, I am grateful. My daughters and sons-in-law were there for me through difficult times, always willing to help in any way they could. I could not have done this without them.

My friends, the Peeps (Ann, Debbie, and Sandy) laughed, sang, and helped bring me through the dark time after David's death. I must also add Bill here – a special thank you to him. Ruth Ann, a life-long friend (well since high school), has always been there for me! Without friends my life would be very less joyful!

To my baby sister, Debbie, a huge thank you! You are one of my most ardent encouragers.

Great thanks to Joyce Mochrie, with One Last Look, for her copy editing. Your words of encouragement and help spurred me on.

30650473R00107

Made in the USA
Columbia, SC
29 October 2018